FRONT COVER: Oxshott, 1910.

OXSHOTT
The Story of a Surrey Village

BY

Dr B. S. GIDVANI
DIC, CChem, CEng. FRSC, FIChemE, FIM

Sponsored by
Graham Clarke, Norman Kaphan & Peter Marsh,
Members of the Federation of Oxshott Residents
and Associations management committee

BARON
MCMXCVI

PUBLISHED BY BARON BIRCH FOR QUOTES LIMITED
AND PRODUCED BY KEY COMPOSITION,
SOUTH MIDLANDS LITHOPLATES,
CHENEY & SONS, HILLMAN PRINTERS (FROME) LIMITED

ISBN 0 86023 572 6

CONTENTS

INTRODUCTION AND ACKNOWLEDGEMENTS

Histories such as this are usually a compilation of information published previously in different places. Often reminiscences of elderly people are included. This book follows that pattern but includes more oral history and hitherto unpublished material. I have considered it especially important to record the memories of as many elderly people as possible before they are lost forever.

Memories, however, are often unreliable and often contradictory. Every effort has therefore been made to check, double-check and interpret the information. Despite these efforts, however, there are bound to be some errors and omissions. If I have omitted or wrongly attributed a fact, I record my regret and apologies.

I have drawn extensively on old issues of the Parish Magazine and found inconsistencies; also old maps, particularly those published by auctioneers. I have also relied on and used unpublished material from Brian Elfick's *The History of Danes Hill*, from B. Fountain's *A History of Oxshott — Roman Times to Present* and the *History of Oxshott* by Class 2 students of the Royal Kent School, Oxshott; my sincere thanks to them all.

My aim has been to make the residents of Oxshott aware of the antiquity and richness of the past of our village. I am conscious of gaps in my knowledge, but hope that somebody else in due course will produce a more complete account. I will be content if I have succeeded in exciting the interest of even a few. Recent housing developments are changing the characer of the village, and no doubt we are passing through an ugly phase, but I look to the vigour, independence and determination of the villagers to protect and preserve their inheritance.

Many people have gone out of their way to give or send information and photographs. To those who gave me their stories and placed their knowledge at my disposal, I offer my heartfelt thanks and apologies to those who are not mentioned. It is not possible to record every name, but I should like to express my gratitude to Timothy Ades who has been a mine of information and a great help. Mike Crute is another who has never failed to dig up old data. My grateful thanks go also to Geraldine Craig for making available old records and photographs, to Mrs Wilmshurst for her late husband's album of postcard photos of old Oxshott and to Roger Deacon for his collection of photos and articles.

I am grateful to the Federation of Oxshott Residents and Associations for undertaking publication of the book and to Peter Marsh, Graham Clarke and Norman Kaphan for underwriting costs, without which the project could not have proceeded. My appreciation and thanks are also due to many friends for their encouragement, particularly to Norman Kaphan and Graham Clarke for their patience and perseverance.

Last, but not least, I am indebted to Nanette Peggie for deciphering my scrawl, typing and re-typing the manuscript. This book will remind her of many hours of unpaid, unrewarded but much appreciated work.

June 1996   B.S.G.

Oxshott Village, 1923.

DEDICATION

To my late wife, Alda Constantina,
without whose initial research, this book
would not have been written.

7

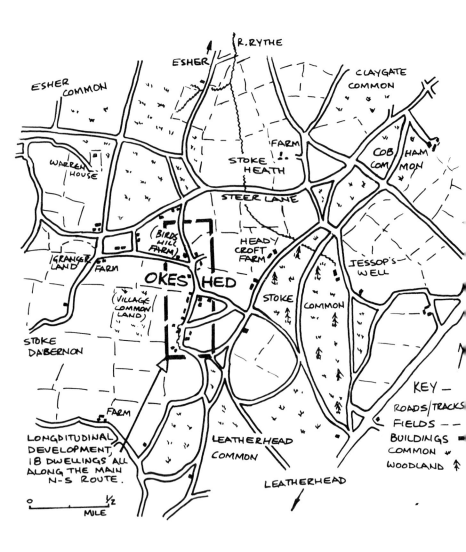

After J. Rocque's Map of Surrey, 1762.

8

FROM THE BEGINNING

'Oh to be in Oxshott,
When the summer's here;
Seated at Hill top,
When all seems far and near'

Kate Ayling

Oxshott is an enchanting village situated within Surrey's
stockbroker belt and on the railway line from Waterloo to Guildford
via Cobham. It lies within a triangle, the points of which are
Kingston upon Thames, Leatherhead and Guildford. It is less than
17 miles from Hyde Park Corner, London and Guildford. It lies
amid pine woods and heathers and is close to the national routes A3
and M25. Heathrow and Gatwick airports can be reached by car in
about thirty minutes. The pleasant towns of Epsom, Esher and
Leatherhead are close by and the villages of Claygate, Cobham and
Stoke D'Abernon are within a radius of five miles. Some 200 years
ago, it was a small clearing in the woods. People lived in huts,
fabricated from timber and straw, with brushwood on the roof and
earthen floors. Oxshott village now consists of mainly luxurious
houses and a High Street which not long ago had busy thriving
shops where ladies dallied to exchange pleasantries and news of the
day. Alas, most of that has now disappeared mainly due to
supermarket development in neighbouring towns and to heavy
traffic which makes crossing the road highly perilous.

Although much has been written about Esher, Cobham and Stoke
D'Abernon, little is to be found about Oxshott. Most history books
ignore it and others dismiss it in a few sentences. It could well be that
there was nothing of archaeological, architectural, historical or
cultural significance to record. The sixteenth century
Highwaymans Cottage, Birdshill Farmhouse and other buildings of
earlier and later periods up to 1880 were not considered worth a
mention in *Old Cottages & Farmhouses*.

However, Oxshott is soaked in history and touched by prehistory.
Samples of sand and gravel from Oxshott Warren are exhibited in
the Geological Museum, South Kensington, representing material
washed from higher ground during the Ice Age. A flint stone was
found by M. J. E. Foulger in the grounds of The Gables, Warren
Lane, which the Department of Prehistoric and Romano-British
Antiquities recorded as 'an irregular flint blade which has been
truncated at one end by steep retouch. It may have been intended

9

as a blank for the production of a burin. Unfortunately it is not possible to give a precise date although the piece is most likely to be prehistoric'. In 1993 a former Oxshott resident, Mr Nicholas Flint, came across a flint on Oxshott Heath said to date back to 8000 BC. It is smaller than the palm of a hand, probably part of the head of a spear left by a hunter which, according to experts at Surrey County Council, is the oldest man-made object ever discovered in the area. These finds indicate a human presence in the Oxshott area eight million years ago. In 1913, five fragments of Roman pottery were dug up in Oxshott High Street.

A circular object found in Oxshott woods in 1935 is displayed in the British Museum. Nearly three centimetres across, it was given by Mr A. Winter in 1955, and is an Anglo-Saxon bronze brooch of the early tenth century. It is intricately carved with 'four small snake-heads on banded necks which meet at the centre', and it was made in England. Alongside are 'a bone button from London with a human figure bound by snakes, a bronze mount with coiled animals interlaced with ribbons and snakes and an iron seax [blade] from Sittingbourne, inlaid with copper, bronze, silver and niello, carved and inscribed'. Such splendid and ostentatious jewellery was greatly prized and clearly belonged to a person of note.

The recorded history of Oxshott can be dated to the time of Edward the Confessor and traced from the annals of Stoke D'Abernon, for Oxshott was a district within it.

During the reign of Edward the Confessor, the manor of Stoke (D'Abernon) was held by *Brictsi* (Brixi), who was a powerful supporter of the king, and also held land in Brixton. The area covered by the manor was 15 hides (approximately 1,800 acres) and was taxed at £4.

When William, Duke of Normandy, won the battle of Hastings in 1066 and was crowned King of England, most of the lands of the English nobility, including that of Brictsi, were distributed among the new King's followers. Stoke was acquired by Count Gilbert's son, Richard Fitz-Gilbert de Tonbridge, Lord of Clare, and it remained in the family until 1314 but a sub-tenancy appears to have been granted in the 12th century to Roger D'Abernon.

Roger D'Abernon of Lisieux, France, was with Duke William in the battle of Hastings and was granted the Manor of West Molesey. Later he acquired *Stoc* (Stoke) and gave his family name to it in 1086. In 1253, John D'Abernon, Lord of the Manor, received a grant of free warren (to kill game) from King Henry III and in the following year his son John claimed an interest in Stoke, which eventual became Crown property in 1418 through the marriage of Lady Anne Neville de Clare to Richard III. Part of the Manor was incorporated later in the Claremont Estate.

In the Manor of Stoke, Richard Fitz-Gilbert also had other land comprising approximately 600 acres which was previously held by Otho from King Edward. There were two villagers with six oxen, and land for two ploughs (a measure of land which could be ploughed by a team of eight oxen in a year). This was probably the small hamlet of Oxshott, in the north-east corner of the Parish of Stoke.

Oxshott's original name is believed to have been Occa's Sceat. *Sceat* is an Old English word meaning strip of land or a corner. Over the years there have been several versions of the name. It was *Okesseta* (1179), *Ockescate* (1203), *Okeosoto* (1205), *Oggesokoto* (1255), *Osckeschete* (1265), *Oxsets* (1275), *Hoggesete* (1281), *Ockechade* (1294), *Occasate, Oggeschate, Hosket, Oggesset, Ogsath, Ogsethe* (all in the 13th century), *Hoogshott* (1313), *Ogcath* (1314), *Hocchessata* (1318), *Ogshette* (1341), *Hoogshott* (1536), *Occasect* (1537), *Oxshott* (1603) and *Ockshot* (1816).

The first reference to the hamlet is in Stoke D'Abernon's Pipe Rolls (Sheriff's accounts) for 1179 as *Okeosots*. There are similar references until 1762 when a map of the *Hundreds of Surrey* was published by J. Rocque, showing the size of the hamlet. A Surrey will of 1603 spells *Oxshott* as now. The name shown on an 1816 map is *Ockshot Street*.

A small manor (administrative area) of Ogshete with a tiny hamlet of a few scattered cottages among woodland lay within the district of Oxshott. Gilbert D'Abernon granted this and the surrounding land, including Oxshott Heath, to the monks of Waverley Abbey. Waverley was the first Cistercian Abbey founded on 24 November 1128 by William Giffard, 2nd Bishop of Winchester upon the banks of the River Wey, two miles south of Farnham. Its ruins, the greatest in Surrey, lie in the shelter of Crooksbury Hill. Although a lot of property, including 35 acres given by Henry III in 1239, was bequeathed to the Abbey, it remained one of the smallest and poorest with a net annual income of £174 8s 3½d (£174.41) which included £4 from *Ogshete*. Since its income was less than £200, it was one of the first to be suppressed in 1536. The property was then granted on 20 July 1536 to Sir William Fitz-William, the treasurer of the King's household, later created Earl of Southampton. Sir William died in 1543 without issue and the estate was divided equally between his wife, Mabel and his half-brother, Sir Anthony Browne, later created Viscount Montagu. Eventually much of it became part of the Manor of Esher & Milbourne.

In Oxshott, there was also a house called Oxshott Grange, probably a part of the monks' holding, owned by the Vincent family in the time of Charles I.

Large tracts of land in Oxshott became part of the Claremont Estate. Clive of India built Claremont House with its beautiful

11

gardens and surrounded it with hundreds of acres of parkland. The Government bought the property in 1816 for £66,000 as a home for Princess Charlotte, the only child of the Prince Regent (later King George IV) on her marriage to Prince Leopold of Saxe-Saalfeld-Coburg. The estate covered 503 acres with ornamental gardens in 6½ acres, a park of about 30 acres, with walled kitchen gardens, stables, etc. A year later the Princess died in childbirth along with the baby who could have followed or replaced her in succession. The distraught Leopold took to travelling abroad but kept Claremont of which he had life tenure with an annuity of £50,000 as part of the marriage settlement. He spent weeks and months there each time he returned.

In spite of his prolonged travels, Leopold maintained, looked after and improved Claremont considerably. He also enlarged the estate by successive purchases of farm and woodlands, a large part of which comprises Prince's Coverts to the east of Oxshott village.

Leopold's widowed sister, Princess Victoria of Saxe-Coburg, married the Duke of Kent on 13 July 1818, gave birth to a daughter (the future Queen Victoria) on 24 May 1819 and was widowed again on 23 January 1820. As a widow, she became relatively poor but Leopold came to her assistance by giving her the use of Claremont where she and her daughter spent much time.

In 1825 Parliament granted her an annuity of £6,000 towards support of her daughter, Victoria, increased to £16,000 in 1831 when she was appointed Regent in 1830.

Leopold was proclaimed King of the Belgians on 4 June 1831. He then renounced his annuity of £50,000 by negotiations with the Prime Minister, Lord Grey, on condition that the State would look after the whole of Claremont Estate and be responsible for the salaries, pensions and allowances of the staff and other employees. But he retained ownership until his death.

Leopold died in December 1865 and the estate reverted to the Crown. But *The Crown Estate — an Historical Essay* published by HMSO (1960) claimed 'in 1865, Leopold I, King of the Belgians, died and left to his niece Queen Victoria for life the house of Claremont in Surrey'. This is incorrect. The marriage settlement of 1816 had only given him life tenure. Moreover, unless Victoria owned Claremont in her own right, she could not have given it later to her son Prince Leopold, Duke of Albany, from whom it was eventually seized as 'enemy property'.

Queen Victoria, who had spent the best part of her childhood at Claremont, was much attached to it and purchased the house with its gardens, parks and some other parts of the estate as part of her personal fortune and became Lord of the Manor of Esher and Milbourne which included Oxshott Woods.

The Crown Estate Commissioners' records contain a letter from one of the tenants who, on learning that the Queen had acquired the Manor, wrote:
'Your Majesty,
Is it true that you are my landlord?
May I say how truly grateful I am?
The rent is already placed in a small tin box (as from 1st June) but how is it to be sent to you is not quite clear'.

In 1882, the Queen gave Claremont upon trust to her young son Prince Leopold, Duke of Albany, when he married Princess Helen of Waldeck-Pyrmont, and the power to grant a life interest to his bride. This he exercised shortly before his death in 1884. That life interest lasted until her death.

The Duke and Duchess of Albany had two children — Princess Alice in 1883 and a posthumous son, Prince Leopold Charles in 1884, who succeeded to the title on his father's death.

On his marriage, the Duke of Albany's allowance had been increased from £15,000 to £25,000 but, when he died, leaving Princess Helen a widow at the age of 23, the Government reduced her allowance to £6,000. As the Queen's youngest daughter-in-law, she found it difficult to keep a house and her high place in society in London. She, therefore, moved to Claremont, transforming it from a palace to a real home for her two children. She engrossed herself in their upbringing and in the welfare of Esher and its inhabitants and in other good works.

Queen Victoria's second son, Prince Alfred, Duke of Edinburgh and Duke of Saxe-Coburg-Gotha, died in 1900 without issue. The Queen decided that her grandson, the young Duke of Albany, should take his uncle's German duchy. In spite of strong opposition from Princess Helen and the young man, he was packed off to Germany to become a 'good German' and loyal vassal of his cousin, Kaiser Wilhelm. This was the making of a great personal tragedy as the Duke had to serve in the Germany army in the 1914-1918 war, while his sister Princess Alice's husband, Prince Alexander of Teck, fought with the British forces with distinction. Prince Alexander became Earl of Athlone in 1917 but the Duke of Albany was stripped of his British honours, titles, distinctions and property rights. In spite of the shock and stress, Princess Helen, Duchess of Albany, a German by birth, remained thoroughly British and devoted herself to British Red Cross and allied war charities. She contributed generously, often beyond her means, so that she had to sell jewellery. She died in 1922 when the Claremont estate legally passed to the Duke of Albany but, as he had been declared an enemy alien in 1917, the property became vested in the Custodian of

Enemy Property. Claremont Estate was auctioned in 1923 and lot No 37, consisting of the Manors of Esher and Milbourne, which included Oxshott Woods, was purchased by Esher Council for £2,000.

The vested property was only the part which Queen Victoria had given as a marriage gift to her son, the Duke of Albany, and the adjoining land, which Prince Leopold had purchased in his own right, was not affected. The Crown Commissioners had already purchased Prince Leopold's land for £91,850 in 1867. That consisted of 1,650 acres and included Arbrook, Stokesheath, Birdshill and Little Heath farms and Prince's Coverts.

The Parish of Stocke (Stoke) was bounded by the Parishes of Cobham on the north, Leatherhead on the east, and Great Bookham on the south. The river Mole separated Stoke from Great Bookham, also from Cobham on the west. There was a vast common with oak trees on clay in the eastern part of Stoke bordering Leatherhead. A fine meadow called Hundred Acres lay on the south side. The soil towards the north east is gravelly and there is good hazel mould elsewhere.

Rocque's map shows the layout of Oxshott. Settlement followed the pattern of time; longitudinal development along a north-south route through a thick forest between Esher and Leatherhead. The route is along a high ridge. There is a farm at each end, Birdshill Farm, and Danes Hill Farm, and up to that time, the expansion was between these farms. The map also shows three other farms on the eastern side of the high ground near a small stream called River Rythe and a building marked Jessop's Well. Only 18 buildings are recorded.

The following table shows the number of landsowners during 1780-1830:

	1780	1790	1800	1810	1820	1830
Landlords	35	34	27	28	27	22

The progressive descrease in the number reflected the absorption of small holdings, leading to fewer large landlords.

The growth of the hamlet between 1762 and 1845 is evident from the Tithe map of 1845. Two of the three farms on the east side are gone and some of the common land has been developed. The population of Oxshott was then 193.

Birdshill Farm gets its name from the family of John Byrd (1593) and Bird (1620). In 1777 the farm was owned by Sir George Warren of Fetcham Park and let to Ann Peacock. A plan attached to the survey carried out by Mr Samuel Driver shows its size. In 1818, it was owned by Prince Leopold and leased to William Wheston. It consisted of 97 acres. By 1861 it had grown to 130 acreas and in 1871

14

it was 145. Similarly, other landlords were buying out small holdings so that, according to the Tithe Assessment of 1836, there were only six major owners — Prince Leopold, Charles Mahon, Captain Smith (probably a son of the then Lord of the Manor of Stoke), the Sheath family, Sarah Arter and Mr Reynard.

Agriculture, forestry and tending hogs were the mainstay of the hamlet up to the middle of the nineteenth century, when gradually sheep and dairy farming took over.

Small farmers had been taken over and some of the land was used for house building. After the opening of the railway station, the process accelerated, so that by 1927 there were only Arbrook, Stokesheath and Little Heath farms left.

In 1638, John Webster farmed Grange Farm, which was Little Heath Farm and which eventually became known as Ayling's after its owner, George Ayling. It extended from Cook's Crossing to the hill beyond Waverley Road, reaching Danes and Wrens Hills. A spark from one of the first steam engines set ablaze the thatched roof of Little Heath farmhouse which at that time was much nearer the station. The farmhouse, together with its outbuildings, was razed. A new farmhouse was built in 1886 near Cook's Crossing. The farm had not only the farmhouse and outbuildingts, but also a number of cottages for farm hands. Some of these were destroyed during the Second World War and rebuilt in the 1950s.

Then there was a small Friesian herd, which grazed the fields off Blundel Lane. Traffic was held up when the cows were brought to the farm for milking and some thought them 'an anachronism'. At first milk had to be collected from dairy farms but later H. & T. Prewett of Manor Farm, Stoke D'Abernon, delivered twice daily from a churn on a horse-cart.

Ayling was not too keen on machinery. Milking was by hand and ploughing by horses. Only harvesting was by a hired mechanical harvester.

Repeated compulsory acquisitions by the local council reduced the size of his farm to under 50 acres, which he considered uneconomical. He sold it to a Mr Ruff who was connected with the Surrey County Council. The Friesian herd was replaced with Jerseys. Mr Ruff, too, found farming unprofitable and sold out. The farmhouse remained vacant and soon became derelict. It was later demolished and the land used for the houses of the Oxdowne Road.

The 'new' section of Blundel Lane joining Steels Lane to Cook's Crossing, built in 1935, was originally part of Ayling's orchard.

Since Oxshott was not a separate entity, separate population figures were not recorded. However, the population growth in the Parish of Stoke, which includes Oxshott, was as follows:

	1791	1811	1821	1831	1841	1851	1861	1871	1881	1891
Population	290	307	317	289	352	335	368	356	408	527

	1901	1911	1921	1931	1941	1951	1961	1971	1981	1991
Population	571	722	848	1,031	[No Census]	2,926	4,951	5,555	5,405	5,220 (Oxshott 3,000)

There was no school and no church, the nearest being the Parish Church in Stoke D'Abernon, a mile and a half away, and seldom accessible in winter. The villagers spent most of the time on Sundays, either in the Bear Inn, nick-named 'Oxshott Church', or sitting on farm stiles while the children played and quarrelled.

The Bear Inn was the first public house, opened about 1776. It was in an old cottage standing end-on to a narrow country lane. It also had a forge and a blacksmith's shop. Sarah Arter was the licensee in 1841, her son-in-law William Smithers in 1861 and his son Robert in 1871. The next landlord was Sayers and after that Fred Taylor. During the 1914-18 war, on Government orders, his storage space became the coal depôt. People came at all hours to collect coal whch meant he had to leave the bar. When the war was over, Mr Taylor bought a donkey-driven cart to deliver coal. His brother assisted him. Neddy, the donkey, was strong-willed and difficult to harness, but worked well. However, he would not move without his daily pint of ale. All the patrons were aware of his habit, and would occasionally, out of mischief, 'treat' Neddy to an extra pint or two with disastrous results. He would either not budge except to kick the front of the cart or become sleepy and lie down, still harnessed. Fred Taylor's son, Stanley, who was born at the pub in 1908, recorded that once Neddy was so impatient for his pint that he tried to rush into the bar and the cart got stuck in the door. Unharnessing was out of the question for fear that Neddy would create havoc. With effort, ingenuity and patience, they managed to release both Neddy and the cart.

Stanley took over from his father and was landlord until 1936. Wallaker was in charge from 1936 to 1955, followed by Steer for the next sixteen years to 1971.

The present public house was built in 1925 at the rear and then the old Bear was pulled down. The owners at the time were Messrs Hodgson of Kingston upon Thames. The present owners are Young's Brewery, London, and mine hosts are Geoff and Christine Young.

During the second half of the nineteenth century and early part of the present one, the Bear was the starting point for local hunts, fox hounds, drag hounds, harriers, beagles, etc. Often there were two meets in a week. With the development of the village and the building of residential properties, the hunts gradually faded out.

Annual auction sales of locally grown timber were held at the Bear until 1942.

After retiring, Stan Taylor continued the coal business from Bembridge, his home opposite the Church in Oakshade Road. He also had a coal depôt facing the railway station. Bembridge was built in 1898 and is one of the earliest surviving buildings in Oxshott.

Stan was chairman of the Royal Kent School's Parent-Teachers Association and of Oxshott Men's Club for some years and, on retirement from that office, was made an honorary vice-president for life.

Another inn, the Queen Victoria, was opened in 1787, and up to the mid-1840s was only a shed in front of a cottage with a rough long table and chairs. Isaac (Puller) Sheath was the landlord in 1841, his widow Mary in 1851, and their son, William Sheath, from 1881 to the late 1890s. It is not recorded when the word 'Queen' was dropped. The present building dates from 1850 and was extended in the 1980s. Isaac Sheath also owned a farm near Pond Piece.

Stag hunts met at the Victoria. A horse-drawn van containing a stag would arrive, accompanied by huntsmen with hounds, and a number of ladies and gentlemen suitably mounted and attired. The stag was let loose, and allowed to reach Prince's Coverts along the fields, before the hunt started. When the hounds caught up with the stag, they would be called off and not allowed to kill. The same stag was used for following hunts.

The Victoria was also the stopping stage for the four-horse stage-coach on its way to Dorking. 'A tall figure in a drab cape, long cloth coat, and tall, shining hat would stand up in his seat on the top of the coach, then on a long horn would announce their arrival. A scene not to be forgotten. The coach usually stayed at "The Vic" for a spell and customary refreshments.'

Roads were once non-existent but there were tracks wide enough for a cart. Colonel William Mudge's Ordnance map of 1816 has a tiny section marked Ockshot Street with a road between Esher and Leatherhead, ending in open ground marked Leatherhead Common. Presumably there was a path across the Common to Leatherhead.

Earlier maps do not show any direct route between Leatherhead and Esher. The track past Danes Hill appears to go through fields (now Birds Hill Rise and Birds Hill Road), turns right just where Steer Cottage is, and continues as a little track to Stokesheath farmland. This eventually became Fairoak Lane and Stokesheath

Road. Part of it continues through woodlands to Epsom. Fairoak Lane remained a cart track until 1925. The present direct link between Oxshott and Esher *via* Warren and Copsem Lanes was made early this century.

An alternative route to Leatherhead is also marked, which is now Oaklawn Road. It was used by villagers to go to Church at Stoke D'Abernon but, during dry weather, many made their way across the fields.

Oxshott was connected to Stoke by another track starting at the top end of Steels Lane and reached by crossing a stile. Farley Lane was the name of the upper part (up to the Church) of this muddy and potholed track across meadows and a swampy area strangely called Wapping Dock where a Baptist Church was built in 1873. The track was named after Edward Farley, who had rented the small corner plot, where the Church car park now is, from Thomas Sheryer. Farley also owned and worked a field at Sheath Lane next to Pond Piece. He also had a field in Steels Lane where Arnewood now is. The land belonged to Francis Woodhatch, who also owned the site of Clock House Mead and the Clock House, and was acquired when the land was enclosed by Act of Parliament in 1821. The Clock House was built in the 19th century, presumably by Woodhatch.

About the same time, Prince Leopold purchased some of the land of Little Heath Farm, land in Sheath Lane from Thickets to Little Heath Farm Cottages and Red Lodge.

Farley's Lane is now Steels Lane, named after the Mr Steel who succeeded Farley. Along the lane were two old semi-detached cottages demolished about 1920 and a little further along, two more semi-detached cottages, one of which housed the local policeman. Rose and Oakshade Cottages have been claimed as these two cottages. The only other houses in the lane were the Orchard and an old house replaced by the Clock House early this century. Still further along was the Little Heath Farm House with its thatched roof, and then around the bend came Little Heath Common. Mr Mottram, who weighed almost 30 stones, lived in the farmhouse. When travelling by railway, he had to use the guard's or goods van as he was too big to get into any compartment. When he died, his coffin had to be lowered from a bedroom window.

Coffins were usually carried to the burial ground in Stoke, but sometimes placed on a farm cart manually hauled.

'Diggers', after forcible removal from common land between St George's Hill, Weybridge and Cobham, set up a makeshift camp on Little Heath in 1650. There was a pitched battle to evict them. The Diggers, sometimes called the True Levellers, were followers of Gerard Winstanley, who many believe was the father of English Socialism.

A track connecting Oxshott to Cobham through Little Heath Farm is also shown on the map, but it was usually impassable in bad weather; even cattle sank to their knees in clay mud and had to be pulled out. Perhaps Oxdowne gets its name from that. The sharp bend of the track is now Brown's Corner.

Most of the paths, tracks and lanes were named after people whose houses they served, or across whose fields they went. Blundel, Goldring, Sheath, Steel, and others were prominent residents. Some of the names are descriptive, for example Broom Hall was a mansion of that name on Broom Hill, Copsem Lane is from Copseham Farm, Birds Hill Drive, Rise and Road are from Birdshill Farm, Danes Way from Danes Court Estate, Pond Piece from a small pond on the site, Princes Drive from Prince's Coverts, Warren Lane from Sir George Warren, Waverley Road from Waverley Abbey, Cook's Crossing from the adjacent brickworks of John Early Cook, and so on.

Brown's Corner gets its name from the Brown family who kept two shops at the Cook's Crossing end of Littleheath Lane. The shops were in Pinewood, an Edwardian house with two entrances. The grocery/greengrocery had the door on the same side as the crossing and the door for tobacco, cigarettes and confectionery was on the Littleheath Lane side. All the 'laners', as the poet Barbara Garner calls them, went there not so much for the goods they supplied, but also to meet the Browns. They had always lived in Oxshott and were full of stories and reminiscences. Jack Brown was known as Jack and his wife Evelyn was always Norah. Jack's three sisters, Maud, Mabel and Violet (Vi) made up the family. Mabel worked in London and, after her retirement, occasionally gave a hand in the sweet shop. Jack and Vi served in the grocery and Maud and Norah in the confectionery and tobacco shop. Vi was an expert in locating and distinguishing edible fungi on Oxshott Heath. This was the tuck shop for the boys of nearby Reed's School. Maud often exhibited paintings at the Arts and Crafts Society's shows.

They are now all gone, and so are the shops. Norah died in April 1984 aged 81, and the funerals of both Mabel aged 84 and Violet aged 79 took place on 21 June 1989. The house has been modernised and enlarged. Brown's Corner, as it was, lives only in memory.

ABOVE: HRH Princess Charlotte. INSET: Anglo-Saxon
bronze brooch from Oxshott Woods. (Photo by Godfrey
New, Westminster Library)

LEFT: Prince Leopold of Saxe-Saalfeld-Coburg, (after the picture by Sir Thomas Lawrence). RIGHT: The Duchess of Kent with her daughter, Princess (later Queen) Victoria (from a drawing by Sir George Hayter, 1834).

ABOVE: The Duchess of Albany with her children
Princess Alice and Prince Leopold Charles, (*Strand
Magazine*, 1834). BELOW: Little Heath (Ayling's) Farm,
1966.

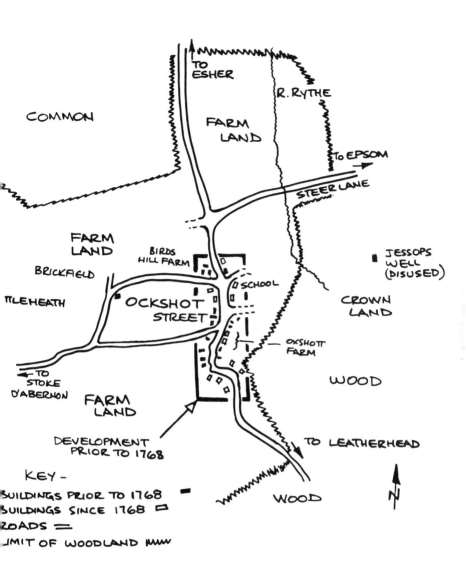

Oxshott — After Tithe Map of Surrey, 1845.

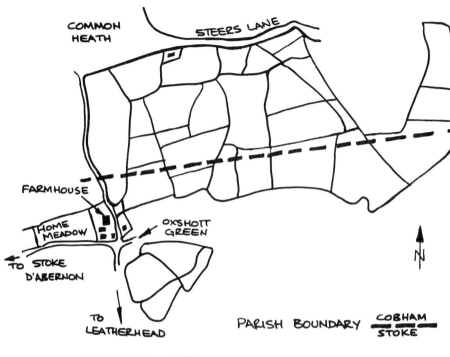

ABOVE: Plan of Oxshott (Birdshill) Farm by Samuel
Driver. BELOW: Derelict Little Heath Farmhouse, 1967.

24

ABOVE: The (old) Bear prior to demolition c1923, and
BELOW: the new Bear, 1995.

ABOVE: Oxshott Hunt 1904. BELOW: The Victoria, 1910.

26

ABOVE: The Victoria in 1995. BELOW: A view of
Ockshott, Surrey, c1816.

ABOVE: Farleys (now Steels) Lane, 1906. BELOW: Brown's General Store, corner of Little Heath Lane (now Brown's Corner).

VICTORIAN VILLAGE

In 1877, Oxshott hamlet was still tiny with only 29 scattered cottages. The hamlet proper consisted of Birdshill Farm buildings with a large barn which had been used as a school in 1818. There were cowsheds with galvanised roofs sloping right down to the footpath. In the severe winters common in those days, icicles would hang from the roofs which the school children would break off and suck with relish. On the opposite side of the farmhouse, there were two cottages which belonged to the farm and a single-storey primitive cottage built about 1830 with only one large room and a kitchen, followed by a pretty cottage on the corner, occupied by Mr Almond, the head keeper of Prince's Coverts. Then came the Royal Kent School and the master's house surrounded on three sides by an orchard. There was a cottage in the middle of the orchard in which a Mrs Skelton lived and sold sweets. After the schoolmaster's house was the hamlet's only shop, started by Albert Charles Napper, where he sold groceries and home-made bread baked in an old fashioned brick oven. Next to the shop was his coal yard and then the Victoria public house.

The hamlet received its post *via* Leatherhead. The arrival of the postman was an event. Weather permitting, he would walk from Leatherhead, otherwise use a bicycle. He would blow a whistle to announce his arrival. The villagers then met him to collect and/or hand over their mail.

Soon after the opening of the railway station in Oxshott, Napper's shop was extended and two cottages built between the extension and the Victoria. Oxshott's first post office was opened in the front room of the cottage next to Napper's with Frederick Skelton as sub-postmaster. Letters on weekdays (Saturday, in those days, was a full working weekday) came from the main post office at Leatherhead at 7.05 and 10.00 am and 7.00 pm and were despatched at 8.00 and 10.50 am and 7.10 pm. On Sundays, the arrival was 7.30 and the despatch at 10.30 am. Post in the evenings and on Sundays was for collection only. With no vans and by foot or on bicycle despite foul or fair weather, the villagers had a better service then than now.

Later the post office was transferred to Napper's, who by then had sold out to A. J. Manser. When the telephone system reached Oxshott, Manser was the first with Number One, also used as a public telephone.

Manser had obtained an off-licence to sell beer and other alcohol. He was the village's grocer-cum-greengrocer and fruiterer-cum-off licence-cum-post office. After the Second World War, Manser sold the business to A. Cotterell & Son but not the sub-post office. That was transferred to the shop adjoining Oakshade Road which was built before the war. W. H. Cullen bought the business in the 1950s and were in turn taken over by Dillons in the mid-1980s. The post office was transferred to them so that it was (and is) back in the old premises of the nineteenth century. The shop with the post office is now owned by Mr and Mrs Chandegra and trades as Arkays.

The second cottage was a private house with its front room used as a haberdashery. Later the business changed to a butcher's shop. A slaughterhouse was built behind the cottage. Bert Hastings was the first butcher. A. Hartshorn, who had a similar business at North Street, Leatherhead, took over and closed the slaughterhouse. After several years' trading as butchers, he sold out to Grimditch and Webb. They carried on well into the seventies and then sold it to the Vestey Group who traded first as Matthews and then as Cobb. The business was closed down on 19 September 1992. Michael Baker, who had been the manager for several years, was transferred to Cobb's Cobham branch.

Oxshott was without a butcher for almost a year when Frank Crossley reopened the business. Crossley was compelled to close down and once again the village had no butcher. After about a year, Crossley once again reopened, but then suffered a heart attack and the village was left without a butcher for another spell of nine months. Messrs P. J. Dale and J. Harding, family butchers of Hampton Court, reopened the shop in January 1996.

Facing the school across the road was the village green and a pond where the villagers laundered and hung out washing, and boys slid on the frozen pond in winter. There were no buildings on that side up to Highwaymans Cottage which was built in 1548. It is alleged that Dick Turpin or some other notorious bandit lived in the cottage. Since Turpin operated mostly in the Nottingham area, it is unlikely, but that some bandit occupied it is credible, as nearby Portsmouth Road was one of the favourite haunts of robbers. No signs remain of the tunnel to the Bear which was supposed to be the escape route. The land from Steels Lane to the Bear, including the site of Highwaymans Cottage and all that now is Broom Hall and the Ridgeway belonged to C. T. Mahon. Mrs Carl (Betty) Wallace, who was associated with Mrs Doris Helen Duvivier, lived at the cottage during the early 1940s.

After the cottage came Oakshade House, now called Oxshott Lodge, built in or before the 1850s. Samuel Bradnack ('Dr

Grimstone'), a well-known Wesleyan missionary, led services in its dining hall in the late 1850s. Thomas Cuvelje lived at the lodge until Dr T. C. Blackwell arrived at the turn of the century. At one time Oxshott Lodge was the home of Mrs Olney, a sister of Walt Disney. Canadian officers were housed there during the last war.

Further away is an old cottage called Cartref, where the district nurse, Mrs Lizzie Davies, lived. Some distance away was an old barn, and then comes the Danes Hill Farm House where Rev Edwards, chief chaplain to the Royal Air Force, lived. He was followed by Dr and Mrs G. B. Hollings, and it is now the home of Mr and Mrs Bruce Caporn. The farmhouse is a listed Class II building, built in the early sixteenth century. It is a half-timbered house with heavy oak beams black with age standing at the entrance of what was then Oakshade Farm. Its timber frame is infilled with whitewashed bricks with a plain tiled roof hipped with gablets. It has one of the now disused wells which provided water for the village.

Beyond was the Bear public house and a farm with a cottage occupied by Mr Willoughby. At the back of the Bear, there was an old house and a pathway towards Wrens Hill, ending in the bridle path to Blundel Lane. Mr Cox lived in the old house. He was the proprietor of the famous Slaters Restaurant in London and lost his wife in a horse-riding accident.

Willoughbys Cottage and the farm were acquired by Alfred Williams early in the 1900s. The farm was between Hunters Moon and Britla. Mr Williams built the Willoughby mansion with outhouses, stables and a dairy. His head gardener was William Gray. Mr Williams was chairman of the Old Parish Council and president of the Oxshott Horticulture Society in 1919. Mrs Williams for many years helped Dr Barnardo's Homes and opened her house and grounds to raise funds. She was also active in the Mother's Union. The mansion was requisitioned in 1940 for billeting Canadian officers. Mr Williams moved to Sidmouth where he died in 1942.

In 1945 the Willoughby mansion was divided longitudinally down the middle and converted into two large dwellings named Willoughbys East and Willoughbys West, each with its own spacious landscaped garden. The original vegetable garden, orchard (felled in 1965) and the old vine house now form Willoughby's Nurseries. The Porter's Lodge, Willoughbys Lodge, still stands within its own garden at the entrance to the drive of Willoughbys East on the Leatherhead Road.

The stable block and dairy have been converted into two semi-detached houses known as Willoughbys Croft and Torresdene. These are surmounted by the splendid original clock tower, recently restored to working order by the present occupant of Willoughbys Croft. This is a well-known landmark for all who approach Oxshott from the south. On the north side of the old tiled stable yard stands the original Coachmans Cottage.

Within the boundaries of Willoughbys Nurseries lies the 19th century farm building which was converted into a dwelling house in 1946 by the addition of a matching gable within the walled farmyard. The ancient farm wall, reduced in height, now encloses the sun terrace of the house on what was once the midden and pigsty. The farmyard wall and the old part of the house must be among the oldest in Oxshott. The house is appropriately named Willoughbys Farm and has been the home of R. A. H. Arnold for the past 40 years.

Continuing towards Leatherhead, after Willoughbys, there was the Charlwood Farm of about 100 acres, owned by Capt Smith and farmed by William Sanders. After the Second World War, a building estate was developed in Charlwood Drive.

On the other side of the road, there was a small farm of about 25 acres belonging to Prince Leopold and leased to Darius Chilman. The farmhouse facing the Bear was occupied by Baron White, probably a son of R. Baron White (Ginger Beer White) of Robin Hill. During the last war, the house was occupied by a Mrs Derrit whose husband served in the Navy. There were cottages too, named Danes Court Cottages. Number one was the home of Mr Letts, the head gardener at Danes Hill farm house. All these have been replaced with new houses in Old Farmhouse Drive.

In 1780, on the opposite side of the road almost facing Wells Cottage, there was a house named Oaklands which was demolished and a new house with the same name built for Lord Justice Sir Charles Butt in 1888. Later its name was changed to Danes Court. It had several cottages, farm buildings, large stables and extensive grounds, including the pond near Meadway. The property was acquired in 1899 by James J. Morrish who lived there until his death in 1919.

Mr Morrish supported Oxshott in every way. His daughter and two sons, Guy and Ralf, like their father, worked for the benefit of the village. Mr and Mrs Guy Morrish lived at Hill House, Birds Hill Drive until his death in 1920. Later Mrs Morrish moved to Orchard Cottage and lived there until her death. She was honorary secretary of Oxshott Women's Institute in 1920 and president in 1930. Ralf moved to Cobham.

Alan Ansell purchased Danes Court from Mrs Guy Morrish. He owned property in Surrey but lost it all in 1924. Soon after, a ladies finishing school was started. Rodin Cottage was the only house in High Drive, which was just a grass path in the early 1900s.

The village obtained its drinking water from a number of wells. A survey carried out during the Second World War revealed that most could be reactivated if necessary. One of the wells is in the grounds of Beverstone, Birds Hill Rise. Oxshott gets its water now from the East Surrey Water Company at Redhill.

Groceries mainly came from Platt's Stores, Kingston upon Thames. They sent a travelling salesman once a fortnight to take orders and deliveries were made two days later.

Highwayman's Cottage, built c1548.

ABOVE: The butcher's shop, c1909, and BELOW: vacant
in 1995.

ABOVE: Willoughby Clock Tower. BELOW: Bridle Path
with Mr Cox's house.

ABOVE: Danes Court, 1959. BELOW: Wigmore's Tea
Rooms, 1906.

MIND AND SPIRIT

Education came to Oxshott in 1818 when it was still a tiny hamlet of about 200 inhabitants mainly consisting of small farmers and day-labourers. Most lived in primitive cottages with earthen floors, open to the roof. They toiled all day, growing corn, wheat and barley, lopping trees and tending cattle and hogs. Their only relaxation was at the two inns, the Bear and Victoria. There was no church or school. They could neither read nor write.

A letter from a Leatherhead resident, 'A J' to Rev T. Wilson in 1818 commented on the pitiable conditons in the hamlet; the inhabitants were 'a poor, and too, too long a rude uninstructed people . . . Without any means of instruction, they lived in a state of deplorable ignorance and depravity, having within themselves neither church nor chapel, nor school of any description. The parish church [Stoke] is two miles and a half distant, which, in winter, is seldom accessible in any manner. On this account, the public house at Oxshott being the most frequented of any on the Sundays, has, for half a century, been known by the name of *Oxshott Church*. On the day which Divine appointment seconded by the law of the land, has required us to keep holy, this house was filled with devotees of drunkenness and riot. There the wretched peasantry, to use the expressive language of one of them, since made sensible of the evil, 'soaked their lives away' — there, lost to all sense of moral good or evil, and seemingly unconscious of a God and another world, they wasted their scanty earnings on intemperate indulgences, ruinous alike to soul and body . . . God Almighty was never wanted in any place more than at Oxshott'.

'A J' felt that this state of affairs was intolerable. He approached the church warden. They considered that a start could be made with a Sunday school. The vicar of St Mary's and others supported this. Mr W. Wheston offered to lend a barn in one of the fields in Birds Hill Farm, now the site of the car park next to Birds Hill Farmhouse.

Barn School. The barn was cleared of corn and cleaned and on a Sunday in June 1818, the Barn School was born. Fifty-two children were enrolled on the first day, 48 of whom did not know the alphabet. Parents, being illiterate, were unable to help. Arrangements were made with a number of ladies to teach childen in their private homes, 'dames' schools', but the problem was that the teachers themselves had difficulty in reading. They had to spell many words several times to themselves before they could

37

pronounce them properly to their pupils. Teaching was limited to the three Rs and readings from the Bible. The school, however, was a huge success, and within a year the numbers had grown to 100 — more than the barn could accommodate. The school was closed for enlarging and a gallery, seats and heating were installed. It was re-opened after a week, Rev J. Knight of Kingston upon Thames performing the ceremony.

The barn was used as a chapel on Sunday evenings. Reverends Atkinson, Churchill, Knight and Whitehouse from neighbouring villages and towns preached there.

Children at the Barn School made such quick progress that they could read the scriptures in four months. Girls were quicker to learn than boys. Not to lag behind their children, many of the parents requested to be taught and an adult school was started. Farmers were against adult education as they considered that it would spoil peasantry as 'beasts of burden'.

The rapid progress is attributed to the efforts and devotion of a foreigner, a young Swiss from Canton Vaud who had come to Leatherhead to improve his knowledge of the language. The local clergy helped with religious instruction, but he did most of the teaching. He assisted parents, visited the sick, and poor and lonely and befriended the wealthy who helped the school financially. He became 'Pastor' as well as 'Teacher'. He was the founder of the Adult School in Oxshott.

Royal Kent School. Numbers still grew and a provisional committee was formed to build a proper school. It obtained the support and patronage of HRH Prince Leopold of Saxe-Coburg and his sister HRH the Duchess of Kent, who resided at Claremont in Esher.

Hugh Smith of Manor House next to St Mary's, Stoke D'Abernon, offered land opposite the green for a school building. He gave a lease for 199 years from 29 April 1820 at an annual rental of sixpence to Robert Bateman Wilkins and Alexander Jardine, appointed trustees. The land was to be used for building a schoolhouse for 'instruction of children of poor persons in reading and writing, and for preaching of the Holy Scriptures and instilling moral duties to be used also as a place of worship or chapel for the preaching of the Gospel'. The Kuwait petrol station now stands on the site.

It was decided that the school would operate on the principles of the British and Foreign School Society — a voluntary national society whose main function was to open schools throughout the country and train teachers. It had established about 100 schools including those at Chertsey, Dorking, Godalming, Guildford and Kingston upon Thames.

A single storey building with three classrooms was erected with primitive toilets and a row of washbasins under an awning at the rear. Water often froze during winter. Although the school had capacity for 80 children, there were no more than 50 pupils at a time; the population of the village was 350.

The school was formally opened on 16 October 1820 by the Duchess of Kent accompanied by her brother, Prince Leopold. It was named Royal Kent School after the late Duke, who had died only nine months before. Both Prince Leopold and the Duchess of Kent gave £25 each in addition to £50 which the Prince had already contributed.

The public meeting before the opening ceremony was well-attended by gentlemen, ministers, and Messrs J. Millar and Allen, secretary and treasurer respectively of the British and Foreign School Society. Prince Leopold thanked and congratulated Mr Wheston for giving up one of his barns for over three years to the Sunday school which had led to the new institution. Chairing the meeting the Prince said:

'Ladies and Gentlemen,

The object of this meeting is the establishment of a Day-School at Oxshott, for the benefit of the children there and in the vicinity. These children were most decidedly in want of such an institution, the peculiar position of their habitations being at some distance from any place where schools exist. The present establishment, in the central situation in which it stands, will therefore prove highly beneficial, as the children have shown great anxiety to profit by the means of information, which a Sunday school had already afforded them. I therefore beg leave to recommend most earnestly this new institution to the warm support of this meeting'.

He then went on to commend the merits of public education, and concluded:

'Real piety is the only support in adversity which never fails, when no other consolation can avail. I speak from sad experience, and may say, that without the support of religion, I could never have borne the unexampled calamities with which it has pleased Providence to visit me'. His wife, Princess Charlotte, had died after only eighteen months' marriage.

Then followed a longish report by John Burrell, secretary of the Provisional Committee. A number of resolutions including the following three were passed unanimously:

'1. That a Day School be established in this place, for the benefit of the children in the Hamlet and its vicinity, to be called the Royal Kent School, Oxshott,

'2. That the Royal Kent School be founded and conducted on the following principles:

(a) That this School be opened to the children of persons of every religious denomination; for which purpose the reading lessons shall consist only of extracts from the Holy Scriptures, in the authorised version, and that no book, commentary or interpretation tending to inculcate the peculiar tenets of any religious denomination shall be introduced into the School on any pretence whatever, (b) that the children be taught reading, writing and arithmetic, according to the system of the British and Foreign School Society, with the addition of needlework for girls, (c) that all subscribers of half-a-guinea annually and upwards, or donors of five guineas and upwards, be members of the Society for conducting the business of this School, and be eligible to become members of the Committee, (d) that the subscribers be entitled to recommend in rotation, one child for every half-guinea subscription, and three for every guinea subscribed, (e) that the children admitted into the School be required to pay one penny per week, or sixpence per month, unless the Committee shall find, upon enquiry, that the parents are unable to pay the same, in which case they shall be admitted free.

'3. That the following gentlemen be a Committee for the year ensuing:

Robert Barclay (Bury Hill), J. H. Butcher (Cobham); John Burchell (Letherhead) *sic*; Joseph Burchell (Letherhead); A. Dendy (Dorking); James Dixon (Letherhead); R. Ironmonger (Effingham); Joseph James (Esher); J. Millar, Secretary, British & Foreign School Society (London); Charles N. Palmer (Kingston); H. Peto (London); J. Peto (Cobham); Joseph Sayers (Dorking); J. Toriano (Oxshott); W. Wheston (Oxshott); R. B. Wilkins (Jessop's Well); Secretary: John Burrell (Letherhead); Treasurer: W. Alers Hankey (London).'

Hugh Smith and William J. Denison MP were elected President and Vice-President respectively. Prince Leopold and the Duchess of Kent agreed to continue as Patron and Patroness.

The Barn School was closed and all its activities transferred to the new building. Children received lessons every day and on Sundays were taught the Gospel. Adult classes were held in the evenings. The rebuilt barn was demolished in 1960.

One of the classrooms was licensed for public worship and a full service was held every Sunday evening at 6.30. Service was also held every second Sunday morning at 8 o'clock. A harmonium was used for accompanying hymns, which after some years was replaced with a small organ.

40

The establishment in 1820 of a school in a small hamlet was a memorable event for Oxshott. In the whole of Great Britain in 1818, only one in every 17 children was attending a school of any sort and, even in 1937, only fifty-seven per cent of the entire population could read and write. Government started financing education only from 1839 when Parliament voted £30,000 for the whole country. The Oxshott school did not see a penny of it, but was fortunate to have the patronage of Prince Leopold and the Duchess of Kent and others.

Little is recorded of the school's early days, not even the name of its first headmaster, but it is believed that the popular young Swiss of the Barn School volunteered. It made steady progress and some years later, a small two-storey, four bedroom house was attached to the building for the schoolmaster.

The school fell on hard times a few years later. Hugh Smith died on 29 April 1831 and his son, Rev Hugh Smith, became Rector of St Mary's, Stoke D'Abernon. He was a pluralist, with the livings of St Mary's and of Weston Subedge in Gloucestershire. Rev Smith neglected Stoke parish and visited it only occasionally. He withdrew the financial support from the Royal Kent School.

Prince Leopold left Claremont on becoming King of the Belgians on 16 July 1831. His financial support to the school ceased too. Enthusiasm elsewhere waned and contributions dwindled. The school faced serious financial difficulties and had to close in 1836.

Soon thereafter, the vacant premises were vandalised and windows smashed. A squatter named William Joseph took over. Howitt vividly describes the hamlet: 'This is the village of Oxshott. Go through it on a Sunday when the agricultural people are at leisure, and there they are as thick as motes in the sun, in the middle of the village. There appears to be no Church, nor any inhabitants but farmers and labourers. Boys, girls and women, all seem to be out of doors, all in their everyday garb. The boys are busy enough, playing at ball and cricket. The men seemed to pass their time, sitting on the banks and stiles, or gossiping and smoking in groups. Scarcely a soul will move to let you pass. The intellectual condition of this obscure hamlet is strongly indicated to any passers through, by a large school and house founded in 1820; but which since was so confounded, that its windows are broken to atoms. This state of things should not be allowed to continue. The vast wealth of the aristocracy living here and about, do not accord. There are many, no doubt, who would be anxious to secure an education for the local children.'

Fortunately another benefactor came along in 1859. He was Rev Phillips. His mother, a widow, had acquired Manor House in 1831 (renamed Stoke House in 1850) when her son was 13 years old.

Frederick Parr Phillips, born in November 1818, was a grandson of Phillipe Egalité, Duc D'Orleans and a half-brother of King Louis of France and inherited considerable wealth. He entered the ministry in 1831 and was a curate at St Lawrence's, Hougham, near Dover from 1841 to 1851. Rev Phillips purchased the advowson of St Mary's, Stoke D'Abernon in 1852 but under the then prevailing ecclesiastical law, could act only as a curate during the lifetime of the rector, the pluralist Rev Hugh Smith. Rev Phillips was appointed Canon and Rector on Rev Smith's death in 1862.

Soon after becoming curate, appalled by the poverty, ignorance and illiteracy of his parishioners, he decided to reopen the school in Oxshott. To do that, he had first to get rid of the squatter and that was no easy matter, as the law in those days allowed squatters after a number of years' continuous occupancy, to claim ownership. It cost Rev Phillips £50, a large sum at that time, to persuade William Joseph to leave. He spent more money on repairs and enlarging the adjoining schoolmaster's house and undertook to maintain the building and pay staff salaries and other expenses. He had the lease of the land and building transferred to himself. The school was reopened in 1859.

Children had nowhere to play except in the street (cart track) and on the green facing the school. The Canon bought the orchard behind the school as a playground. In the midst of the orchard was a timbered cottage with a thatched roof where Mrs Skelton lived and sold sweets. Her son became the verger at St Andrew's.

There was a green corrugated iron hut on the other side of the school, which Rev Copson Peake, resident curate in charge of Oxshott, had transferred from his home at Danes Hill. Up to 1910, it was used in the afternoons for confirmation classes, mothers' meetings, etc, and in the evenings as a meeting hall. It was also used by Miss Verrey for carpentry classes for boys and later became the scouts' hut. Across the path, where now stands the telephone exchange was a pond, where children skated.

After Canon Phillips' retirement in 1892, the Hon Rev Noel Waldegrave (later Lord Waldegrave) became the Rector, who in turn was succeeded in 1897 by Rev A. S. P. Blackburne. Both continued the good work of Canon Phillips in Oxshott. However, Canon Phillips continued to bear all the expenses of the school until 1902, when the Surrey County Council became responsible under an Act of Parliament. The Council had to pay for the teachers, books, equipment, lighting and heating and maintenance of the buildings, but the land and buildings remained vested in the owners. The supervision was entrusted to committees of local managers which, in the case of Royal Kent School, consisted of Rector Rev Blackburne, B. A. Bristow, Basil Ellis, R. J. Lambert, J. J. Morrish and F. A. Phillips.

Subsequent vacancies on the committee were filled by G. G. Vertue (1908), F. M. Halliday (1908), Mrs Bowen Buscarlet (ex-widow of F. A. Phillips who died tragically in an accident in 1911), Rev F. N. Skene (1914), Mrs Verrey (1914), R. A. Dash (1916), Miss Alice Grey (1919), Ralph Morrish (1919), Guy P. Morrish (1919), Rev N. G. Davies (1921), L. H. Shadbolt (1921), J. Tilley (1921), Mrs Trinder (1925), Mrs H. F. Taylor (1930), Mrs O'Brien (1937), Rev T. J. C. Ford (1938) and Rev R. S. Lound (1942).

Canon Phillips, according to J. J. Morrish, was short but of generous girth. In his surplice, he resembled 'un petit Mont Blanc'. However, he was a pious man of great kindness and cared for his parishioners more than for himself. It is said that on wet and stormy nights, he would sit with an open umbrella in front of the marble fireplace in the great hall of his manor and, when urged to have the house re-roofed, would mildly reply 'It will last my time'.

One of his friends was John Early Cook of Little Heath Brick Works and Knowle Park. Another was Henry Hansard of the parliamentary records journal. Canon Phillips was inclined to be long-winded in his sermons. There were occasions when Mr Cook took out his gold pocket watch two, three times, sighed heavily and snap-closed it, murmuring 'too long, too long'. The Canon would then skip several pages.

Canon Phillips retired in 1892 but continued his good work and was chairman of several charities. Chairing a meeting in 1902, he reported that he had failed to find a person to attend the sick in the parish for a retainer of five shillings (25p) with extra payment for each case undertaken. He was appointed an honorary Canon of Winchester in 1894 and Rural Dean of Leatherhead. He died in 1903 aged 84. Among his papers was a note saying 'I ask forgiveness of any I have pained or injured. I remember gratefully the kindness and forbearance of my parishioners and ask them to think with indulgence of my many shortcomings. May this Parish be prosperous and happy'. The Canon left investments of about £650 for the education of village children.

Frederick Abbis Phillips of Old Parks was the only son and heir of Canon Phillips and inherited all his properties, which included the school. By an indenture dated 4 May 1903 he, under the authority of the Schools Sites Act, voluntarily conveyed the school property to the vicar and churchwardens of St Mary's, Stoke D'Abernon, upon trust. Thus the school became the Church of England Royal Kent School. When the new parish of Oxshott was established with its own church, the property was transferred by a deed of 19 October 1914, to the Incumbent and Churchwardens of the Chapelry of St Andrew, Oxshott.

The managers were unpaid. They were responsible for recruitment of teachers, salaries, equipment, books, maintenance of the buildings, etc. The annual grant from the County Council was based on the number of children attending the school and was, more often than not, inadequate. Managers' time was spent trying to find money for repairs and improvements. A school inspector reported that during a period of three weeks in February and March of that year, on only two days schoolrooms had a temperature exceeding 58°F at 2 pm. Even the ink froze in the inkwells.

Some of the Minutes are revealing. An assistant mistress felt it her duty to report that 'the Headmaster appeared to be suffering from mental trouble as evidenced by delusions and a very peculiar manner'. An investigaion proved her right and he was sent off on a prolonged leave of absence. It is not recorded if the poor chap ever recovered and returned.

Another headmaster overslept on most days and arrived late. He would take his breakfast behind the blackboard.

Most of the children were from local families of tenants and employees of the large estates, Bevendean, Broom Hall, Danes Hill, Knott Park and others. The school continued to prosper and, as the village grew with the arrival of the railway in 1885, so did the number of pupils. It was extended in 1897. During World War II, school children had to cross the road to use the air raid shelter built on the green triangle facing the school.

The Education Act of 1944 abolished the 'non-provided' status of schools and made the county councils responsible.

Surrey County Council expected Oxshott to expand rapidly after the 1939-45 war and envisaged a population exceeding 4,000 needing a school for 160 children. It had concluded by 1947 that a new school on a new site in Oxshott was a must, but it was only after the school had become 'controlled' in 1952, that a site was sought. In the meanwhile, overcrowding meant the headteacher had to teach a class of 30 and the infants' class was usually some 25. Parents frequently complained and organised petitions for a new primary school. The old school site had several other disadvantages. It was only about half an acre. The playground was small and the school had no hall. The children had to eat dinner at their desks.

Surrey County Council, after consultations with the Borough (Esher Urban District) Council's Schools' Managers and Parent-

Teacher Association, selected the present site of about 2½ acres in Oakshade Road. The influencing factors were its central situation, almost midway between the High Street shops and the Church, on a road almost devoid of heavy traffic and, as the school was to be built in two stages, nearness of the old and new parts would ease difficulties of administration. There was strong opposition from the site owner and others.

Albert E. Wilson had purchased Meadow Gate in 1948 for £8,000, with about 3 acres of land. Less than a year later, he bought nearly nine acres of adjoining parkland with its sloping fields and abundance of old oak, elm and other mature trees to give 'a fine outlook and preserve amenities' of his home. He refused to sell the land and suggested other sites at Clay Plantation, the junction of Blundel Lane and Waverley Road and Holtwood Road. The County Council rejected these proposals and issued a compulsory purchase order in July 1954. Mr Wilson organised protests and appealed. Among those opposing were Vicar Rev Herbert Evans and R. C. Tarring, secretary of Oxshott Village Sports Club. A public inquiry was ordered by Sir David Eccles, Education Minister, and conducted by S. D. Greaves. The inspector's recommendation not to site the school in Oakshade Road was overruled by the Minister and the compulsory purchase order was confirmed.

A co-educational school was built for 160 children and 30 infants. William T. Bishop was Chairman of the Managers Committee. The new school was opened on 2 September 1958 with 147 pupils. Since only one section of the building had been completed, huts were erected for classrooms. A whistle was used until parents purchased the old school bell at an auction in the 1960s. It now stands mounted on a plaque over the steps to the front door. Games were played in the ground of the Sports Club. The transfer was supervised by the headmistress, Miss Thora Hutt, who succeeded Miss Gladys Mays in September 1954.

Within seven years, the building had to be enlarged for two more classrooms, but that proved inadequate and hutted classrooms are still in use. At present the school has accommodation for 240 pupils. The school badge was designed by E. F. Huit of The Ridgeway.

When the eleven-plus examinations were abolished in the 1980s and middle schools introduced, it was expected that a new building would be provided for 320 pupils aged 8-12 and that the Oakshade Road building would become the First School. However, the scheme was dropped for lack of funds. The Royal Kent School became the First and Middle School in September 1976. Middle Schools were abolished in 1990 and the school is now a primary school catering for children aged 5-11.

The old school building in the High Street was purchased for £10,000 by Rowland Weller of Wellers Garage, Cobham, who also owned Oxshott Motor Works next door to the schoolmaster's house. The school building was demolished in 1969 but Rev Copson Peake's hut remained untouched. Mr Weller sold the two properties to the Kuwait Oil Company. The garage was closed on 14 April 1978 and demolished the following month. At the same time digging started on the old school site for the Q8 Petrol Station.

Since the reopening of the school in 1859, there have been several headmaster/mistresses, but the records do not reveal the first one. George Stoton was in charge from 1888 to 1909. He was assisted by his wife and daughter and Miss Kate Ayling. Kate was a pupil at the school and was designated Pupil-Teacher and appointed a full teacher in 1915. She left in March 1917 to teach at Mr Cook's iron hut school in the brickworks.

Mr Stoton was called Daddy Tot. He was a popular figure and active in parish and community work, taking Sunday school, assisting Oxshott's resident curate, Rev Copson Peake, conducting the choir and playing the organ at the Sunday Evensong held at the school. He was also the organist on Sunday mornings at St Mary's, Stoke D'Abernon. He was a prominent member of the cricket team. His son William was in the local choir and also sang with the choir of the Chapel Royal, London.

He continued to live in the village after his retirement in 1909 and helped his daughters at their haberdashery shop at No 4, the High Street. Mr Stoton was hon secretary and/or treasurer of most local charitable organisations.

Miss Thora Hutt was a teacher when the school was still in the High Street. She was a capable teacher and administrator, kind, compassionate and yet firm. She had her own house, Oak Tree, facing the school in Oakshade Road. Her health deteriorated after being bitten by a dog, and she retired in July 1973 after 40 years' teaching career.

The headteacher now has a complement of 12 full and part-time teachers.

Bevendean School. Mrs F. Haines of White Garth in The Ridgeway was the founder of Bevendean Preparatory & Nursery School in 1936. It was so named as it was on the Bevendean Estate. Mrs Haines had been headmistress of an elementary school in East London and after taking an early retirement at the age of 50, she decided to start a Nursery and Preparatory Day School in Oxshott for boys and girls aged 4 to 10. She approached the Commissioners for Crown Lands for a plot of land at the end of Goldrings Road to put up a modern

46

rectangular building with a flat roof but her proposal was turned down. However, she was persuaded to take a lease on the old Bevendean Laundry adjoining Steels Lane. The conversion was entrusted to Alan D. Reed FRIBA, who had previously won a public competition for designing a school in North London and was responsible for enlarging and modernising Bevendean Lodge for W. Bishop CBE. It would have been hazardous for children to cross Steels Lane as there was no footpath adjoining the north side of the Bevendean Laundry, so an access footpath from Holtwood Road was built.

Mrs Haines decided to cater for both girls and boys and arranged her school in groups — a nursery group for children aged 3½ years to five years, a kindergarten for five to six years old and a junior section for pupils between the ages of six and 10 years.

The school opened in September 1936 with only five pupils, one of them Robin, son of Mr Bishop, but soon attracted more and employed Margaret Hamilton, a Froebel trained teacher for nursery classes, Mrs Marion Boyle for languages, and Miss M. E. Smith for music and eurythmics.

Mrs Haines was succeeded by Miss Margaret Hamilton and Miss O. C. Weaver as joint principals and later by Mrs Manning.

Mrs Manning persuaded the financier Jim Slater, whose children were pupils at the school, to set up a charitable foundation, the Bevendean Trust, to purchase it. After Mrs Manning's retirement, Michael Binney was the headmaster.

Bevendean School continued independently until July 1982 when Graham Hill, Headmaster of Danes Hill School, bought it. The latter was until then for boys only but, after the amalgamation, it became co-educational for children from three to 14 years old. The amalgamation was inaugurated when J. A. Attenborough, Headmaster of Charterhouse, unveiled a specially designed clock built in the main building of Danes Hill.

Bevendean School building in Steels Lane is now used as the junior school.

Danes Hill School. Joseph Hendy-Morton acquired in 1947 a Crown lease of Danes Hill Mansion with its vast grounds with the intention of establishing a preparatory day and boarding school for boys aged seven to 13 years. He had some interior modifications carried out and advertised for pupils in 1948 with himself and T. J. Powell-Shehan as joint principals. Later Rev Francis Brown joined them. F. R. H. Beven took over from Mr Powell-Shehan in 1950. He lived at Danes Croft, Leatherhead Road and was a cricket enthusiast. The school prospered and soon established a reputation for both teaching and sports. In 1952, there were 61 pupils and some had won scholarships to public schools.

47

Mr Hendy-Morton left in 1953. J. S. Beckett, whom Mr Beven had known since his student days at Brighton College and at that time Head of the Junior Department of Kings College, Taunton, became joint principal. Rapid expansion followed. The old dairy gave way to a new entrance and driveway in 1953. An opportunity came to widen the drive on the north side when the 1987 hurricane toppled several trees and weakened many more. The school attracts students from Oxshott, Claygate, Cobham, Leatherhead and Stoke D'Abernon.

Messrs Beven and Beckett retired in 1969 and a partnership of Messrs M. T. Bolan, T. G. Hill and J. E. Todd took over. Mr Bolan was one of the teachers at the school since 1961 and Mr Hill had been a student there. However, Mr Todd after a short period returned to his native New Zealand.

Expansion continued. Leases of Wren's Hill and Ridgeway Field were purchased to provide improved playing grounds. Planning consent was obtained in 1974 for new buildings to provide for up to 650 pupils. Boarding was abandoned in 1975 and in 1980 a lower school for boys aged 4+ was started in a separate purpose-built unit. In 1982 it purchased Bevendean School in Steels Lane. Up to then, the Danes Hill School had been boys only but with the amalgamation with Bevendean, it became coeducational, catering for boys and girls aged four to 14 years.

The combination led to further progress and Mrs Hillary Elfick of Wybarton, Moles Hill, investigated raising the age limit to 16, but, before this study was completed, the school was purchased in 1984 by the Davies Educational Trust, London, now the Vernon Educational Trust.

The Davies Educational Trust was established in 1975 and owns several preparatory schools, colleges of further education and international colleges.

Graham Hill left in 1984 to join his family boat-building business. R. J. Hadman, an ex-teacher at the school, was appointed headmaster with Mr Bolan as assistant. Mr Bolan teaches chess, and the school in 1987 provided a quarter of the Surrey team which won the England Primary Schools Chess Association Championship. Mr Hadman retired in 1989 and Robin Parfitt was appointed to succeed him.

The school now has approximately 680 pupils. A new building called 'The Ark' was completed at a cost of £600,000 to provide new halls for drama, music and gymnastics. The opening ceremony was performed by Dame Angela Rumbold MP in June 1994.

School fees in 1954 for day students at Danes Hill were £28 17s 6d (£28.87), by 1970 had increased to £90 and now range from £244 to £1,702 per term.

In summary, Oxshott has two primary schools, one private and the other State controlled. The curriculum in both schools is almost identical. Apart from the fees, and size of classes, there is little difference. The private school has a higher teacher-pupil ratio. There is no secondary education in the village. After the age of 11+, children are schooled in Esher, Leatherhead, Epsom, Cobham, Guildford or Wimbledon.

Danes Court Domestic Science School. Miss S. B. Proctor and her sister, Mrs James, acquired the lease of Danes Court and founded a ladies finishing school for boarders aged 16+. Miss Proctor was the resident Principal and Mrs James held examinations.

The front part of Danes Court mansion with the main staircase became private quarters. The nursery and staff quarters at the back with separate staircase provided accommodation for the girls. Staff had their own cottage. There was a squash court and a grass tennis court. The ornamental gardens and park had a kitchen garden which supplied fresh produce.

Several upstairs rooms and bathrooms had iron bars on the windows which were allegedly put there to prevent the young ladies fraternising with Canadian soldiers quartered at neighbouring mansions.

There were thirty girls at a time and ten new girls accepted each term. The course lasted one year and the girls were trained in all aspects of housekeeping and entertaining.

The school continued until 1959 when the lease ran out and was not renewed. Danes Court was demolished, but many of the trees in the park were preserved. The site was developed for housing. The estate is now known as Fern Hill.

Margot Conrade School of Dancing. Although there was no dancing school in Oxshott till 1954, dancing classes for children have been held in the village since the end of the First World War. Mrs Sally Ades, now in her seventies, recollects attending dancing classes in Reverend Mikellatos' time at Bevendean House, when she was about seven years old. Miss Paddie Hackett of Crispin Cottage, Leatherhead Road, a teacher of dancing in Cobham, gave lessons. However, it was Margot Conrad of Spring Waters, Silverdale Avenue, who established a school devoted exclusively to ballet dancing. She is a member of the Royal Academy of Dancing.

Starting with 'tinies' (from 2½ years old) her classes progress through all grades of the Royal Academy of Dancing and major student training. Pupils are prepared for entry to the Royal Ballet School and several have gone on to the Royal Academy College, for teaching qualification. The school is a founder member of the recently established Surrey Region of the Royal Academy of Dancing which meets regularly at Guildford University.

49

ABOVE: The Barn School, 1817. BELOW: Royal Kent
School 1820; the taller section, the Headmaster's house,
was added later.

50

ABOVE: Royal Kent School, 1895 (Kate Ayling with Mrs Stoton standing on far right), and BELOW: in 1907 with (standing left) Rev Blackburn, (far right) Mr & Mrs Stoton.

51

ABOVE: The Green Hut. CENTRE: The old Royal Kent
School and BELOW: the new Royal Kent School in
Oakshade Road, 1958.

First day opening of Royal Kent School in Oakshade Road
— Miss Hutt welcoming the pupils.

ABOVE: Kate Ayling at the age of 93. BELOW:
Bevendean School.

THE RAILWAY

Oxshott's growth started after the railway station was opened. The extension of the railway line from Surbiton *via* Claygate and Oxshott to link up with the Waterloo-Guildford line at Effingham Junction took three years to build. Tons of earth had to be excavated by hand and taken away by horse-drawn carts. During the building of the road bridge at Oxshott, traffic was diverted down Fairoak Lane for about 300 yards, then along a temporary cart track over the heath, to rejoin the main road further along. That track is now Heath Road.

The station was built to the same pattern as Claygate, but with the booking hall and waiting room on the up side. Originally the station was called Oxshott and Fairmile, but the latter was dropped in 1956. There is some controversy as to when the station was opened. According to the *Parish Magazine*, the first train to arrive was on Monday, 2 February 1885, witnessed by a crowd of residents. Walter Tye has recorded that the actual opening of the railway was in 1887. However, all are agreed that Mr Meakle (Meikle) who had joined the London & South Western Railway Company (Southern Railway) in 1879, was the signal man who saw the first train in. He remained at Oxshott until his retirement in November 1927.

The first stationmaster has not been traced. According to A. C. J. (Jack) Punchard, whose father was the stationmaster from 1896 to 1906, there was also a Mr Putman PRS (porter and relief signalman). The signalman at Cook's Crossing was Mr Tucker, who lived in the red brick house beside the line. His signal box is now gone and the crossing is automatic, controlled from Surbiton since 9 September 1973.

About midway between the station and Cook's Crossing, there was another called Sheath's Lane crossing, manned by Edward Bourne, who lived in the adjoining cottage in Sheath Lane. His namesake, Edward Nutcher, grandfather of the local painter and decorator, Michael, succeeded Mr Bourne who, on his retirement, became the head gardener at Englefield. The footbridge was built c1910 but Sheath's Crossing continued until 1967, when it was closed. Thus the staff consisted of four men and the ticket office was open the whole day. Now, there are ticket-vending machines with only 'half' a booking clerk; the office closes at about 1.30 pm.

The steam engines used were the eight-wheeled 0-4-4 tank engines as most other types were considered too heavy for steep gradients. There were eight trains a day in each direction except on Sundays, when there were only three each way. The service had increased considerably within the next two decades. Now it is half-hourly from Oxshott in the morning, starting at 6.13 until 11.43 in the evenings, except on Sundays when it is hourly.

All the station buildings including the stationmaster's house were lit by paraffin lamps and water was pumped up from a well to cisterns for flushing toilets.

Most of the morning passengers were commuters to London. Those who lived at Fairmile walked through the woods and across the heath to the station. In bad weather, they left their galoshes in the booking hall and in winter also their paraffin or candle-lit lamps. The station staff had the lamps lit and lined up with galoshes ready for collection when the owners returned in the evening.

Electrification of the Waterloo-Guildford *via* Cobham line was announced on 6 December 1923 and the formal opening, with a special electric train carrying railway officials and local dignitaries, took place on 9 July 1925. Public service with electric trains started on 12 July with a speed limit of 54 miles per hour, taking 52 minutes to cover the 30 mile journey from Waterloo to Guildford.

A small goods yard was also built near the station for the solid fuel needs of Oxshott. There was a cattle loading bay at the Cobham end of the up platform. The goods-handling facilities were discontinued in 1959.

Coal carried by the railway and passing through Oxshott had to be weighed in accordance with the Coal Duties Act 5 & 6 of William & Mary's reign. The London Coal & Wine Continuance Act 24 & 25, 1861, imposed additional duties for the relief of 'orphans and other creditors of the City of London'. The Act provided *inter alia* duties of four shillings per ton on all wines and four pennies on each chaldron (a coal measure of 36 bushels) of culm (coal dust) brought into the Port of London. The duties were additional to those authorised by the Coal Duties Act. However, the additional duties were restricted to the Metropolitan Police District. The Act provided for the erection of boundary marks. A cast-iron obelisk carrying the City of London Arms with lettering 24 & 25 Vict. C. 42 marks the boundary and can be seen near the railway line adjacent to Stokesheath Road, a few yards from where the southerly boundary of that part of Claygate which formerly was in the ecclesiastical parish of Thames Ditton, crossed the railway line. The obelisk is a Grade II listed structure.

White-painted cast-iron posts were erected on all roads going into London. Two of them can be seen on the Oxshott-Esher road — one near Sandy Lane, and the other just before the by-pass roundabout. Other Coal Tax posts are in the lane to Arbrook Farm, in Birchwood Lane and in New Road. The original orphans' fund was continued long after its objects had been achieved and in the end was used for other purposes, including building, improving and maintaining of Blackfriars and other bridges and the Holborn Viaduct.

With the opening of Oxshott station, Londoners found Oxshott Woods within easy reach. Day trippers and organised school parties were a common sight at weekends. Schoolmasters allowed the children to roam the woods and play on the heath. Napper sized the opportunity to cash in by providing luncheons, teas and other refreshments in a marquee. As the business grew, so did the marquee, which eventually could accommodate up to 300 persons for a 'knife and fork' meal.

Sometimes the children were caught in the rain and got soaked. There was nowhere to shelter other than the station. The station staff would take them to the waiting room and light a fire to enable the children to dry out. Mr Punchard, the stationmaster, would then arrange for special trains to get them back to London and usually each child was given a bun and an orange to eat during the journey, all at his expense.

The Bridge over the railway.

ABOVE: Oxshott Station, 1904. BELOW: Cook's
Crossing, 1908.

ABOVE: Cook's Crossing in 1973, and BELOW: after automation.

ABOVE: Sheath Lane Level Crossing and Footbridge.
BELOW: Scovell's Tea Rooms.

THE HIGH STREET

A block of three shops, with living accommodation above, was built around 1895, starting at the corner of Oakshade Road going towards Esher. The corner shop was Wigmore's tea-rooms. Wigmore also operated a coal distribution business from the premises. The centre shop was J. Scovell's confectionery, tobacconist and stationery. Finally, the small draper's shop was run by Miss Priscilla Stoton and her sister; their schoolmaster father helped now and then after retirement.

Some years later, Scovell started serving luncheons, teas and other refreshments in competition with Wigmore on the first floor of his premises. B. S. Thake acquired Scovell's business in the 1930s and the post office was transferred to him from Manser's. Later, Thake took over Wigmore, closed the catering business in both shops, separated the post office from the confectionery and tobacconist section, and added the distribution of newspapers and magazines. The corner shop became the post office. So it continued until 1964 when Thake sold the corner shop to Mays, the estate agents. The post office was moved back to the centre shop with tobacco and confectionery. At about the same time, Thake more or less retired and appointed a manager. The business was sold in the late 1980s to Dillons on the other side of the road and the post office is now back in the ancient building of over a century and half years. The premises are now used by the Royal Dry Cleaners, who are associated with the dry cleaners of the same name in Thames Ditton. A florist business is also operated from the premises.

Mays continued to operate the estate agency from the corner shop until 1985, when the business was sold to Nationwide.

When the Misses Stoton retired, their haberdashery business at the end shop of the block was acquired by Gwendoline Smith (Oxshott) Ltd, who had a similar business in Ashtead. They expanded the business to include ladies and children's wear, lingerie, foundation garments, fancy goods and wools.

Gwendoline Smith sold the business in the 1970s to Norah Strudwick who continued to trade until the lease ran out. The premises were vacant for almost a year and then they were used for a kitchen planning design service. It is now occupied by Messrs Babayan Pearce, Interior Design.

The block of shops is now a century old and the exterior has not been altered except that the balconies have been removed to extend the living accommodation.

Another block further down was built towards the end of the 1960s. It consists of five shops with flats above and is now called Heath Buildings. The first one was a carpet and floor covering shop. After a few years, it closed and the premises became Mays' accounts office. It continued so even after Countrywide took over from Mays, but recently it has become vacant.

The next shop was and remains, a hairdressing and beauty parlour called Boulevard, followed by a shop which has changed hands and type of business several times. At present it is the Village Ceramics supplying tiles, bathrooms, accessories, etc. It was originally a ladies' dress shop. Next was Willy Hanlam, the ironmonger who stocked everything and has given way to Webster's Gallery, selling original paintings, pictures and prints.

Finally there is a mini-supermarket which fulfils an essential function. It has changed hands several times and became Rayburn Stores. The manager was Martin Hutton, who was there for over 20 years. It is now the Mei Lin Chinese antique shop.

The block of shops facing the Victoria was built in two stages. Two single-storey shops were built in the early 1930s by H. G. & A. Osman Ltd on land acquired in 1925. Flats were built above a few years later. The corner shop was first occupied by an artist who specialised in designing currency. He used the premises for storage. After about 18 months, it became Osman's electrical appliances showroom and repairs shop which was later divided with Osman moving to the back with an entrance in Oakshade Road, and the front becoming a restaurant. Osman, however, retained a small display window.

Osman sold the electrical business in the late 1980s to Morton Samuel, who had an electrical appliance and repair shop next to Everest, the newspaper shop in Steels Lane. Mr Chew was the first owner. A 'cycle business was added later. A few years later, Mr Samuel died and his widow closed the Oakshade Road premises and consolidated the business in Steels Lane. The Oakshade Road premises are now occupied by Trenchard Arlidge, the independent estate agents.

The restaurant was called the Oak Tea Room and was opened by Mrs Goss, who was not a resident of Oxshott. She gave the business to her daugher, Dinah Skelton who, assisted by her aunt, Mrs Brown, made the restaurant a favourite haunt for local ladies.

Dinah married Mr Crick and two years later an Italian restaurant took over. That lasted less than a year, then came a Bangladeshi restaurant named Raja. Marlon Brando ate there when staying at

Copsem Manor. The proprietorship changed a number of times, and the restaurant is now called Deedar Tandoori Restaurant.

The second shop became, and still is, Hélène, the ladies hairdressers. It was started and run by Mrs Doris Helen Duvivier of Aberleigh, Birds Hill Road. Mrs Berridge, the Doctor's wife backed the venture, and Mrs (Betty) Carl Wallace of Highwaymans Cottage was also involved. When the flats were built above the shops, Doris's mother, Mrs Reid, lived there.

Miss Glover (Mrs Mitchell), bought the business from Mrs Duvivier, and soon sold it to Mrs Jordan in the 1950s. Roger Deacon, the present owner bought Hélène from Mrs Jordan in 1972.

The next two shops were built after the Second World War. The end shop, Number One, was the fishmonger, A. F. Pepper Ltd, who also stocked poultry, game and frozen food, and was also the delicatessen. Messrs Capels (Modern Fruiterers) Ltd were the greengrocers and fruiterers in Number Two.

In 1959, Roy Pointer Ltd bought both businesses. Roy went daily to Billingsgate and Covent Garden markets and Mrs Robin Brown managed the shops.

When the lease expired in the 1970s, increased rent made the business unprofitable and Pointer closed.

Unwins, the wine and spirits merchants, are the present occupier of Number One and Present Surprise, a gift delivery shop, are in Number Two.

In the early 1930s, Charlie Newman set up a bake house at the back of Manser's grocery shop, reached by a narrow passage between the garage and Manser's. He was assisted by his daughters and a son. Newman and his family lived at Dorothy Cottage in Steels Lane, which was originally a smithy.

Newman delivered bread by a horsed cart as far as the Tilt and used a hand-pulled cart for more local deliveries. He kept the cart in Manser's shed and horses in the stable of Danes Hill Farm House. Albert Watkins, who worked for Manser's, recalls the day when bread was being loaded, and the horse already harnessed. At the sound of a horn from the local hunt, up went the horse's ears and off he cantered, scattering bread to right and left until the cart stuck in a gate. Newman did not know that his horse had been trained for hunting. The bakery is no more. Charlie Newman was also the village barber.

Towards the end of the nineteenth century, enough wealthy people had settled in Oxshott to support a garage to service and repair their motor cars. A three-storey building with a pseudo-Tudor facade and a workshop at the rear was erected between the headmaster's house and Napper's store. The workshop and the front room comprised the Oxshott Garages Ltd. It had a kerbside swinging-arm petrol pump which held up traffic whenever it was in use. The garage was set up by Mr Arslett, once Mrs Arnold Trinder's chauffeur, but was owned by Rowland Weller of Cobham, who had a similar business in the Stoke Road.

In the 1950s there was a fourth attempt in 40 years to build a by-pass for Oxshott, which would have gone through the grounds of the garage and run at the back of the shops and the Victoria, emerging at High Drive to join the main road.

The Council bought the required land from Mr Weller but not the private houses, which were blighted until the scheme was abandoned in the mid-seventies. The Council sold the land back to Mr Weller at a substantial loss who later sold the whole business to the Kuwait Oil Company which had already bought the adjoining old school building. The garage and the school were demolished and there is now the conspicuous Q8 filling station.

Barclays Bank has been in Oxshott for almost a century. It started life here in 1899, in a first floor room in the three-storey garage building. Later it moved down to a ground floor room behind the garage office. The bank moved to its present picturesque premises in 1965 when Mays of Oxshott, the estate agents, moved across the road. Opening hours at the beginning were 10.30 to noon daily except Saturday; today they are 10 am to 1 pm.

Mr Wood bought the post office cottage, transferred the post office to Manser, and opened the first pharmacy in the village. He lived on the premises. After about twenty years, came J. E. Williams, who remained the village pharmacist until 1971. He too lived above the shop. Then Mr Hepworth enlarged the pharmacy but it was taken over by Southmark Shops Ltd of Leatherhead. A manager was put in charge. In 1984 Miss Janice Pauline Simpson took over, a knowledgeable and helpful pharmacist.

With the arrival of wealthy people, Col. F May, who had an estate agency in Westcliffe-on-Sea, considered it opportune to extend his activities to Oxshott. A small, pretty hut was built in the space between Manser's Store and the first post office cottage, for F. May & Son Ltd. Later the agency became known as May's of Oxshott. It operated from the same premises for almost sixty years and then in 1965 moved across the road to the corner premises at the junction of the High Street and Oakshade Road.

Col May was an entrepreneur. Whenever the opportunity arose, he purchased land for development. May's were involved in development of the Ridgeway and parts of Danes Way, Fernhill and Wrens Hill estates. Col May was associated with May & May

(Builders) Ltd of Dorking. After his death, his nephew took over, but soon afterwards sold to Mr Murray in 1957. Mrs Fisher joined the firm before the take-over, and continued to work there.

Mr Murray was a chartered accountant in the film industry and moved into the estate agency when films were going through a bad patch. He sold in June 1986 to Messrs Horner Hill Ltd, who sold on to Nationwide. The business now operates as Countrywide.

Oxshott also has another estage agent — Trenchard Arlidge in Oakshade Road. The firm started in 1935 in Cobham High Street as Miller Trenchard & Co. Harry Miller, a local builder, built houses and Richard Trenchard sold them. After the Second World War, a new partnership between Dick Trenchard and Edward Arlidge resumed the business.

Dick Trenchard retired in 1963 and Ted Arlidge continued on his own until 1981 when he too retired. He lives in Oxshott. The business was taken over by his son, Kevin, who formed a new partnership with Anthony Webb. In 1983 they opened a branch in Oxshott in the old premises of Osman's electrical repair shop in Oakshade Road. It is under the personal supervision of Kevin Arlidge.

Harold Geoffrey Osman was the first to start a building business in the village, in the 1890s. Later Albert, a second cousin, joined him and the firm became H. G. & A. Osman Ltd with registered offices and a builders yard in Steels Lane, where Ashtead & Leatherhead Joinery Ltd are now.

Osmans built the Working Men's Clubhouse in 1904 and bid unsuccessfully to build St Andrew's Church. The first two cottages put up by them in Steels Lane were Trebarwith and Winkfield, also Dorothy Cottages. They were the builders of the old telephone exchange which was next door to the present one. They bought the swamp of Pond Piece off Sheath Lane and built Ben Level and Ben High in 1936-37. By then, Harold Osman's son Geoffrey had joined the firm.,

Osmans were also the village undertakers, but they had their coffins made by Dotheridge and delivered overnight by train.

Towards the end of the 1930s, an electrical department was added with a showroom in the High Street.

Geoffrey Osman was active in the community and much involved with St Andrew's Church. He was an amateur actor and took part in a number of local plays.

Charles Garfield Hussey of Cotswold, Irene Road, was another Oxshott builder with his yard in Copse Road in Cobham. Many of the houses in Irene Road were built by him. One is called Garfield after his middle name. Some of the cast-iron manhole covers embossed with his initials can be seen in the area. During the last war, Mr Hussey was Joint Hon Secretary of the Oxshott Food Growers's Association. He was a Justice of the Peace.

Another builder was Mr Dering, who settled in Oxshott in 1926. He built Holtwood in Holtwood Road in 1935 and some houses in the Crown Estate.

R. Dowling & Co Ltd of Downside have also built a number of houses in the Crown Estate and elsewhere in Oxshott.

There was a large house occupied by Mr Godfree, where Arnewood Close now stands. Laneside was known as Godfree Cottages. Lucy Akerman lived in No 1. In 1903, she opened the village's first newspaper and confectionery shop in the front room. She also stocked cigarettes and tobacco, groceries and sundries such as soap powder and vinegar.

Mr Akerman was the village cobbler and worked in a shed attached to the shop. He repaired not only boots and shoes, but also other leather goods such as saddles and harnesses. When he retired, Tommy Wyles took over and set up his workshop in the garden of his home in Crown Cottages, Steels Lane.

In the 1930s, Geoffrey Osman's aunt, Miss Hilda Crown, built a house in Steels Lane for her grandparents with her own hands and some assistance from the building firm of Osman. The shop front was added much later. The shop is Everest, the newsagents.

ABOVE: The estate agents of 1904, now Barclays Bank in
BELOW: the High Street.

ABOVE: Swing-arm petrol pump and BELOW: Q8
filling station.

OF MEN AND MANSIONS

Oxshott, as Elfick puts it, 'remained a nothing on the road to nowhere', until the arrival of the railway. Then the picture changed rapidly. With its peacefully quiet location amid woods, heathland and farms, and easy access to London, Oxshott became a most desirable village.

Most of the land was Crown property, and the Commissioners of the Crown Estates insisted that large mansions with appropriate outbuildings in extensive ground were built for gracious living. They seldom sold a freehold plot, and the leaseholds usually had a restrictie clause stipulating a prime cost for building the mansion.

Danes Hill, the substantial mansion which is now a school, was built about 1890 for John Fisher Eastwood and his four sons, Frank Bruce, William Seymour, Arthur Edgell and John Charles Basil. Eastwoods were the proprietors of the Eastwood Cement Company. They were familiar with Oxshott and its surroundings as John Fisher had leasehold land at Oakshade Farm for which the ground rent was £13 13s 6d (£13.675) and William Seymour and Arthur Edgell owned the freehold cottage properties, Numbers One and Two, Steels Lane. By combining the properties and purchasing more land, their total holding became about 61 acres. The site had a panoramic view of vast extent and great beauty over miles and miles of thickly wooded country to Box Hill, Leith Hill and the Hogs Back in the distance. The grounds extended to Steels Lane, bordering Bevendean property and Little Heath Farm, and included the land now occupied by shops on the west side of the High Street.

Danes Hill mansion was approached from the Leatherhead Road by a long carriage drive through an avenue of old lime trees whose leafy branches met high overhead. There were picturesque lodges at each end. The mansion had three reception rooms, a lounge, a drawing room, a splendid billiards room, thirteen bed and dressing rooms, and a full complement of offices. There were rose and kitchen gardens, orchard, stables, paddocks, woods and farmland, and pleasure grounds sloping gently to the south and west. Farm cottages and a separate powerhouse for generating electricity were also in the grounds.

The Eastwoods sold land in Oakshade Road to Mrs Adriana Cobbett in 1897 to build the Red House and in 1903 to extend its grounds. Plots were sold in 1898 to Mr Abernethy for Broom Hall and to Robert Proctor in 1899 for Midgarth. All the sales had restrictive covenants that only one dwelling per plot would be built.

Richard J. Lambert bought Danes Hill in 1901 and lived there until his death in 1915. He was the chairman of Lambert & Butler, the cigarette and tobacco company. The Lambert family were prominent in all the activities in the village and they donated generously to all deserving causes. They opened their grounds for horticultural shows, garden fêtes and scouts' camps. Queen Victoria's grand-daughter, Princess Alexandra of Teck, opened a garden fête there in 1912.

Lambert was a sportsman, much interested in cricket and football. He laid out full-sized cricket and football pitches. He was president of the Oxshott Horticultural Society, the Cricket Club and the Men's Club, for which he had given a plot of land together with a handsome donation.

Danes Hill was auctioned in 1916 and Sir Osbert George Holmden lived there from 1918 to 1928. Sir Osbert's head gardener, William A. Letts, lived in one of the lodges. After Sir Osbert, there were two other occupants, Percy Fowler and F. Smith.

During the Second World War, Danes Hill was the headquarters of Messrs Borax Consolidated Ltd who were powerful enough and had sufficient influence to prevent its requisition for the Canadian army. Harry F. Wright located his garage in the stable block and lived above it. Later Mr Wright moved to Danes Hill Farm House. Joseph Hendy-Morton acquired a Crown lease and converted Danes Hill into a school.

Broom Hall was built by George Neil Abernethy in 1898 on a seven acre plot which the Eastwood brothers sold him with a restrictive covenant that only one dwelling at a prime cost of not less than £3,000 would be built, not including the cost of stables and other outbuildings. Abernethy built a grand mansion with an entrance from the Leatherhead Road by a carriage drive with imposing posts, lined on both sides with trees. The drive and the mansion are gone, but the two posts can still be seen. Broom Hall was the name given by Abernethy to the property, presumably because it was on a hill covered with broom.

Mrs Abernethy was the daughter of Sir John Aird and sister to Mrs Basil Ellis of Bevendean.

Broom Hall was the centre of many social activities in Oxshott from 1907 to 1920. Local children, boy scouts and Oxshott residents, rich and poor, gathered in its grounds on 24 May every year to celebrate Empire Day. A Union Jack was unfurled on the tall flagpole fronting the house, a bugle sounded the Salute and three rounds were fired from a cannon in the grounds. The *National Anthem* and *Rule Britannia* were sung. Each child was given a bag of sweets and one orange, then 'dismissed for the day'. Mr Morrish of Danes Court or some other prominent Oxshott resident addressed the gathering. Then there was a party.

Like most other large houses, Broom Hall, too, was requisitioned for the Canadian army. However, Mr Comber, the head gardener, continued to live on the property to tend the gardens and keep 'an eye on the boys'. He moved in 1947 to one of the new cottages built by the Council on land which was an orchard of Little Heath Farm.

After the Canadians had gone, the Council took over the mansion to house the homeless. The property was not relinquished until 1959 but in the meanwhile, the restrictive covenant was amended in 1957, authorising detached private dwellings with garages on a plot of not less than ¼ acre and at a prime cost of at least £3,000 each house, excluding the cost of the land. The property was sold to a developer but remained vacant until planning consent was granted in 1962. The mansion was then demolished and two blocks of maisonettes, totalling twenty dwellings with forty garages, were erected with entry from a new road off Silverdale Avenue. The maisonettes are located in one of the best positions on a hill secluded in seven acres of well laid out and maintained grounds, and yet within a stone's throw of the High Street and about fifteen minutes' leisurely walk to the station. Oxshott Heath and views beyond, up to Ranmore Common, are visible to the naked eye, as is also the floodlit steeple of Guildford Cathedral on clear nights.

Bevendean: This imposing family mansion was built by Sir John Aird's firm, Messrs Lucas Aird & Co in 1898, for his daughter and son-in-law, Basil Pym Ellis. Sir John was the civil engineering contractor for construction of the Aswan Dam and a Member of Parliament for Paddington.

The mansion had 23 bedrooms, four bathrooms, four reception rooms, saloon hall, billiards room and commodious offices. It had telephone, electricity, running hot and cold water and central heating by hot water radiators. There were wine and coal cellars, a photographic darkroom, and a luggage lift from the basement to the top floor.

There were also seven cottages, a laundry building where electricity was generated, well-equipped stables with a glass-covered washing shed and farm buildings. The mansion was surrounded by a magnificently laid out ornamental garden, vegetable garden and parkland. Outside there was a large brick-built store for wood.

The cricket and football ground with pavilions and an entrance from Sheath Lane were within the Bevendean estate. It extended from the railway to Sheath Lane and Steels Lane and covered 44 acres overall. Originally it was smaller and was expanded by Mr Ellis by the purchase of land whenever possible.

71

The laundry building, which now houses the Danes Hill Junior School, was used not only for laundry work but also for a gas-engine-driven generator producing electricity. The laundry was managed by Geoffrey Osman's grandmother, Mrs Andrews, and her husband was in charge of the generator. There was a telephone connection between the laundry building and Bevendean mansion. Andrews lost his job after Mr Ellis's death but soon found a similar position at Knowle Hill Park.

The butler's residence was called Small Lodge but then the name was changed to Vintilla though now it is back again to Small Lodge.

At the entrance to the estate in Warren Lane was Bevendean Cottage, where lived William T. Bishop, chartered surveyor. He worked with Messrs Cluttons, the Crown Commissioners' estate agents, later with Drivers Jonas. After the sale of the Bevendean estate, he was entrusted with breaking up the property into smaller plots and with building Goldrings and Holtwood Roads. He was involved in the work of the Royal National Lifeboat Institution and Trinity House, who are responsible for lighthouses and pilotage of shipping around Britain's coasts. On his retirement from the chairmanship of Oxshott Heath Conservators, Sir Patrick Nairne presented him with one of his water colour paintings of the Heath. It was often remarked 'How did other villages manage without a William Bishop'. He was awarded the CBE.

Separated from the estate by Warren Lane, there was a shoot of about 1,000 acres which included Prince's Coverts, and provided excellent pheasant, woodcock and 'various' shooting. Mr Ellis held the sporting rights.

Bevendean became the meeting place for most social events. The grounds were used for horticultural shows and fêtes. The Duchess of Albany opened the garden fair in 1903. One popular event was a party given by Mr and Mrs Ellis every year for Oxshott children and their parents; often children and their parents from Stoke D'Abernon and Cobham were invited. The Cobham Brass Band played and tea, entertainment, prizes and presents were provided. Cricket and football matches were played in the Bevendean grounds.

When Mr Ellis died in 1907, the Church Magazine of October stated: 'How much that name stood for in Oxshott — in the parish and neighbourhood and wherever his personality and influence was felt — it is not easy to express. His life was so entwined in our affection and so bound up with all the efforts for moral and spiritual and material progress of the parish that we feel in each home a personal and family sorrow as we mourn his loss'.

Bevendean was sold in six lots by auction in 1908 but the mansion and a large part of the grounds, including the cricket and football fields, remained intact. 72

George Harrison's (of Leatherhead Road, Oxshott) great-grandfather, James Johnston, having made a fortune building Shanghai Docks, returned in 1911 to live at Bevendean. Mr Johnston and his large family shared the house with two other families until 1915. In the 1920s it was the home of Rev Davis Mikellatos, who provided facilities for children to learn dancing. The film magnate, Sidney Bernstein, was the next occupier. He carried out extensive alterations.

The property was vacant in the early 1930s and the Commissioners for Crown Lands bought the estate at auction on 6 February 1935. It was divided into a number of plots intersected by Goldrings and Holtwood Roads, and attractive houses with fair-sized gardens were erected. Now, here too, the move is for replacement with smaller 'luxury houses' with smaller and smaller gardens.

The mansion was empty for a time in the thirties and the Crown Commissioners bought it, with its ornamental gardens and grounds, and later sold it to H. J. Cunningham. He commissioned G. Alan Fortesque FRIBA to convert the obsolete mansion into a small house. The mansion was set into the slope of a hillside so that the rooms which made the basement at the rear, became the ground floor at the front. Complete demolition of the building proved impractical due to its deep cellars and solid foundations. Only the top of the house was knocked down and the central structure retained. A new and smaller building was put up on the old first floor and the rooms under the arches were converted into an entrance hall, a double garage, a billiards room, wine cellars and a boiler room with storage for fuel, etc. The house is called Treetops, stands in about an acre of well laid-out garden and has an entrance from Holtwood Road.

Fixtures and fittings and building material of the partially demolished Bevendean mansion were sold separately at another auction on 1 May 1935.

The other cottages and houses in Sheath Lane and elsewhere were left untouched. Some of the houses have survived and still carry Ellis's initials BPE and the date 1894.

Midgarth was the mansion at the High Street end corner of Steels Lane and was built in 1899 for Robert Proctor. It stood in four acres of magnificent ornamental gardens and a huge vegetable garden which reached to Oakshade Road. After the Second World War, the size of the grounds was reduced to less than 1½ acres by first building a house in Steels Lane, then two houses in Oakshade Road, and in the late seventies, Heath Buildings in the High Street, housing five shops.

Mr Procter lived at Midgarth with his widowed mother. He was a famous bibliographer at the British Museum, and has 'the remarkable gift of remembering all the different incunabula he had once seen and of being able to visualise them at will' — a gift which helped him to compile the first classification of fifteenth century books in the Museum. He was also a mountaineer and met an untimely death by a fall into a crevasse in the Alps.

Midgarth then became the home of Mr and Mrs Faulkner. Mr Faulkner was a director of Imperial Tobacco Company, known in those days for its 'Nosegay' brand. He was president of the Oxshott Men's Club. He died in 1924.

During the last war, Midgarth was occupied by the National Employers Mutual Insurance Company of St Mary Axe, London. Most of the staff lived on the premises. Among the residents, there was a land girl named Miss de la Haye who worked on the farm opposite. Some of the staff formed a 'pig club' and Mr Grimditch of the butchers, Grimditch & Webb, slaughtered a pig for them. Then the staff would have a raffle for a piece of the meat. They also had two goats, which went missing one day and probably ended up on their plates, such was the shortage due to strict rationing.

At the end of the war, Magor Cardell, an ophthalmic surgeon at St Thomas's Hospital, London, took over Midgarth and lived there with his wife and three daughters. The Cardell family sold Midgarth in 1951.

Mr and Mrs J. Lawson-Hill were the next owner-occupiers and lived at Midgarth for nearly 20 years. In 1972, they decided to move away from Oxshott and put the property up for sale. At that time, Esher Urban District (Elmbridge) Council were looking for a site to build housing for frail and elderly persons. Mr Lawson sold Midgarth to the Council for £75,000 under threat of a compulsory purchase order. Shortly after, the Council gave itself planning permission to convert the existing mansion into six flatlets and to erect a new building of 24 flats in the grounds with parking space for 15 cars. However, the scheme did not proceed and the planning consent lapsed. Pending a decision, the Council let the property but when the letting became a Statutory Tenancy, the Council had to pay an undisclosed sum for vacant possession. It obtained another planning consent in 1988 to put up 55 bed-sitting rooms for the frail and elderly, but that consent lapsed too under the five year rule. By then the Council had come to the conclusion that social housing was not necessary in Oxshott and decided to sell the site for private housing development. It put in a planning application for six dwellings but, under strong pressure from FEDORA, agreed to reduce it to four. Thus the trees which would have been felled are

74

preserved, and the amenities unaffected. The Council then sold the site with the benefit of planning consent to the Michael Shanley Group. Four two-storey houses have been built and the site is still called Midgarth.

Englefield is the first house on the right in Warren Lane from the station to the village. It was built about 1890 for R. Ashford Dash in about 1½ acres of grounds. It overlooks Oxshott Woods and Heath, and is only a short walk from the village. The property bordered that of Basil Ellis on the west and south sides. Ashford Dash was associated with the Commissioners for Crown Lands and managed to obtain freehold instead of the then customary leasehold.

Ashford Dash was one of the members of the first committee appointed in 1904 to build a church in Oxshott. He was also one of the five members of the Commission appointed by the Bishop of Winchester to advise him on building St Andrew's Chruch and was the warden of the first vicar, Rev F. N. Skene, until 1919 when he moved away.

In 1908, Ashford Dash bought Warren Farm from the trustees of the late Mr Ellis's estate. The farm, comprising about 15 acres of leasehold land, adjoined his property to the top of Sheath Lane, and reached down to Steels Lane, including the land used later for Goldrings and Holtwood Roads.

The next owners of the house were Mr and Mrs Balston. Mrs Balston was the daughter of Mr and Mrs Arnold Trinder of Pinewood House.

Then came Gordon and Mollie Skinner in 1935. Gordon's father was the first baronet, Sir Thomas Skinner, honoured in 1912 for his work with the Hudson Bay Company and for organising finance from the City for construction of the Canadian Pacific Railway. Gordon Skinner headed Skinner & Co (Publishers) Ltd, London, which later became a part of Reed International. He was a Freeman of the City of London and a Liveryman of the Worshipful Company of Merchant Tailors.

Englefield was the Skinners' country home, as they had a flat in Park Lane, London. While Gordon Skinner was absorbed in publishing, Mollie took up farm management and spent more time at Englefield. When war broke out in 1939, Mr Skinner joined the forces and Mrs Skinner took up residence at Englefield. He was wounded and, on his father's death, became Sir Gordon. Their head gardener was Edward Bourne, who lived with his wife in one of the farm cottages. Mrs Bourne worked as a daily at Englefield.

All farms, during the war, were instructed to produce food. Mollie Skinner divided her farmland into three sections — dairy, cornfield and vegetables. She had six Guernsey cows and was allowed to have four land girls. She was also allotted a trustee tractor by the Ministry of Agriculture and given extra petrol allowance.

Since no farm in Oxshott had a threshing machine, Mrs Skinner hired one from Wards of Egham. The machine was powered by a steam traction engine. About 15 tons was the annual yield.

During the war, the top floor of Englefield was requisitioned for Canadian forces and four nurses occupied it. Englefield was not damaged by any of the bombs which fell in the village, one of which did not explode and was dealt with by a bomb disposal squad. However, a barrage balloon, having broken loose from its moorings at Chessington, drifted into one of its chimneys, damaging it extensively.

Mrs Skinner sold the property in 1950 for £2,800 and left the district. She died in 1965.

Mrs Charles Sutton bought Englefield in 1959 and lived there until 1970 when Stuart Mellstrom purchased it. He and his family still live there.

Warren Estate: At the junction of Fairoak Lane and Warren Lane towards the village, the Warren Estate, comprising four mansions, was built up the hill with steep drives from Warren Lane. All the mansions had separate servants' quarters, stables, huge gardens and wonderful views.

The Warren was built about 1898 and was the home of Louis Verrey, his wife and three daughters. He made his fortune from Verrey's Restaurant in Regent Street, London, which he owned. Mr Verrey was a great authority on poultry, one of the founder members of the Oxshott Horticultural Society and its president for some years. He was also one of the founders of Oxshott Working Men's Club, treasurer of St Andrew's Church Building Fund and treasurer of the Conservators of Oxshott Heath. He was a regular worshipper and a warden at St Mary's Stoke D'Abernon. He died in 1916.

His widow and three daughters continued to live at the Warren and helped with amateur theatricals, concerts, church, the Women's Institute. After their death, the house was vacant for some years, and squatters took over. It was demolished in the 1980s together with The Gables, the next door mansion. Blocks of flats called Clarendon Park have been built on the site.

The Gables was the last of the four houses to be built on the narrow strip of land between The Warren and Pinewoods, with extensive grounds at the rear. It was built about 1908 and became the home of Sir Arthur Worley, the first and last Baronet of Ockshott, in 1916, and later of his daughter Sally and her husband Raymond Ades. Sir Arthur was in insurance in the City.

76

Sally Ades was involved in several activities as president of the Oxshott Flower Arrangement Society and a governor of the Royal Kent School. She opened the garden at The Gables, before and after the Second World War — one of the first with flower arrangements in the house — in aid of the National Gardens Scheme.

Remy Ades was the secretary of the Oxshott Horticultural Society. The show was held annually on the first Saturday in September in conjunction with the fête held in the grounds of the Oxshott Village Sports Club.

The fête had a funfair, displays, usually by RAF dogs or police motor cyclists, but finally closed when the fairground people could not make sufficient profit after meeting the high insurance premium against rain.

The Gables was the headquarters for raising money to build the Oxshott Village Centre.

Mr and Mrs Ades sold the lease with about 20 years to run back to the Crown. The property remained vacant until it was demolished. Remy Ades passed away a few years ago and Sally continues to live in Oxshott in Princes Drive.

Pinewoods House was built in 1890 for City financier Albert Knott, and was originally called The Crows Nest. Later, the name was changed to Pinewood Tops and then simply Pinewoods. The name changed again to Pinewoods House when Bertie Rimmer bought it in 1952. The grounds extended to rather more than seven acres and the Jacobean-style mansion is a Grade II listed building.

The property is approached from Warren Lane by a drive. At the entrance is the lodge which Mr Rimmer sold off and is now occupied by Mr Munday, a solicitor who heads the Princess Alice Hospice in Esher.

Pinewoods House, an L-shaped building, was divided by Mr Rimmer into three homes. He kept the main part for himself and sold the middle, called High Pines to Richard Pilling, a shipwright. John Whiles bought it on Mr Pilling's death. The end, named Pine End, which used to be a nursery, was sold to a Mr Bispham, and since 1983 has belonged to John Etheridge. Its front door is at the back. A. Holeshowski bought Pinewoods House in October 1993 and has modernised its interior.

Arnold Trinder had bought the property in 1917 from Mr Knott and lived there with his family until his death. He carried on many of the activities started by Basil Pym Ellis and Richard Lambert. He was president of the Oxshott Working Men's Club and of the Sports Club.

He owned a fleet of ships which helped Great Britain break the German U-boat blockade in the First World War. He was offered a knighthood in 1919, but his reply was 'How very kind of you, but would it be possible to give me instead a railway wagon full of coal?'. This duly arrived at Oxshott Station where, in those days, there was a short length of goods siding, taking off from the main up line on the south side of the station and running into a fair sized brick goods shed. Arnold Trinder died in 1940.

During the Second World War, the Canadian army built huts in the grounds of Pinewoods, close to Warren Lane and to the fence of The Gables.

After the Canadians had vacated the property, Mrs Trinder moved down to West Lodge, still in Warren Lane, and much later to The Ridgeway to be nearer the centre. She supported the Mission to Seamen, and often held an At Home at Pinewoods in its aid. She was president of the Oxshott Women's Institute and of the Oxshott Village Sports Club. She died in February 1968 during her presidential year of the latter.

When Mr Rimmer acquired Pinewoods, he lived there with his wife and two growing sons. Very much the academic, he had BSc and MSc degrees from London University, a diploma in music from the Guildhall School of Music, London and an MA from Bristol University. After the war he was appointed Deputy Director of Education of Lincoln City. In 1951, he became General Secretary of the National Association of Head Teachers which he left to return to academic life at Surrey University where he was instrumental in founding the new Law Faculty. In addition, he joined Chambers in Lincoln's Inn, having been called to the Bar by the Middle Temple in 1953.

Mr Rimmer was a pianist and organist, and his wife was a violinist. He was also a skilled painter, usually in oils. He is best remembered for his work with the Oxshott Music Society. Mrs Rimmer died in 1955 and did not see the results of his work.

He retired in 1978 and devoted virtually the whole of his time to local activities, principally the Music Society which had by this time changed its name to the Oxshott and Cobham Music Society. He died in February 1986 and his younger son, Roger, came to live at Pinewoods House until he sold it in November 1993, returning to live in North Yorkshire.

Roger Rimmer's older brother, George, was a committee member of the Oxshott and Cobham Music Society. He is a solicitor and a corporate management consultant and lives in Grayshott, Hindhead.

Pinewoods House was used in the Hercule Poirot TV series in 1992. Some of the scenes show its battlemented square bay and the beautiful oak panelled gallery.

Robin Hill (Warren Mount), the fourth house on the Warren Hill, was built in 1895 for R. Baron White to the design of Walter Cave. Originally it was called Warren Mount. A house of perfect proportions, it now stands in four acres of gardens. The original grounds extended to Birds Hill Road and covered about ten acres. The house had a wide view and, on a clear day, it was possible to see Epsom Racecourse with the naked eye and horses on the track with a pair of binoculars. There was a winch for hauling heavy loads up to the house from Warren Lane.

Cave was the consulting architect at Whiteley Cottage Homes, Burhill, Walton, and had designed the first two cottages there. He was also responsible for the Berkshire home of Herbert Henry Asquith, the Prime Minister. Cave's best-known building is Burberrys in the Haymarket, London. According to Hermann Muthesius: 'the external appearance of his [Cave's] houses is more successful than Vosey's, his surfaces have a broader sweep and the whole is more expressive. He has built a number of extremely pleasant houses in the Surrey countryside'. (Warren Mount is one of the only two illustrations in Muthesius's book).

Baron White made a fortune from his lemonade and ginger beer manufacturing company, R. White & Sons Ltd, hence his nickname, Ginger Beer White.

The next occupant of Robin Hill was Sir Ernest Spencer, MP for West Bromwich. He was also a JP and Deputy Lieutenant for Staffordshire. He gave evidence to the Parliamentary Committee dealing with the preservation of Oxshott Heath in 1904 and was one of the first nine conservators appointed in that year.

Robin Hill eventually passed to a Mr Stone who was a solicitor and then to Anthony Puckle, the senior partner in a firm of insurance brokers. Mr Puckle sold off three plots of land fronting Birds Hill Road on which three houses were built.

R. J. Reip was the next owner, who lived there from 1973 to 1990 with his wife and two growing daughters 'augmented by two dogs, a cat, three horses, two families of foxes and a family of badgers, not counting deer who had a liking for tulips and the tender shoots of rose bushes'. Mr Reip was the owner of a car parking company, the Centrepark Ltd, which was eventually acquired by National Car Parks Ltd. He was involved in the late Sam Wannamaker's project to restore the Globe Theatre in London.

Mr Reip's application for planning consent to build one house in his grounds was turned down as the Local Planning Authority insisted on higher density. His revised application complying with this requirement was approved. He sold about five acres with the benefit of residential planning consent. Eleven houses have been erected and the estate is named Chatsworth Place. Robin Hill mansion is owned and occupied by Stephen Watson and his family.

Beverstone is one of the first 'smaller' houses built in 1891 on Crown lands in Birds Hill Rise. It is behind the Q8 petrol station and opposite the telephone exchange. Beverstone was erected for the meteorologist, William H. Dines, by Thomas Cubitt, the Victorian building firm who had built large parts of Belgravia, Bloomsbury, Pimlico, and other buildings including the Ranmore Church. Queen Victoria had used the firm for building extensions to Buckingham Palace and the Royal Mausoleum at Frogmore, near Windsor. William's father George was the general-foreman of the firm, and on Cubitt's death in 1855, took over part of it.

George Dines lived at Pyports (The Cedars) in Cobham with his wife Louisa and daughters, Hetty and Emily and son William who became a famous meteorologist and Fellow of the Royal Society.

The Dines family was interested in meteorology and friendly with Miss Caroline Molesworth of Cobham Lodge who kept comprehensive records of the weather. William's interest in the study of the weather started there.

Beverstone was built with a partially flat roof to enable William Dines to erect instruments to measure wind pressure. His work resulted in the Dines Pressure Tube Anemometer, which became known and used all over the world.

Later, he became interested in the upper air and flew kites carrying instruments to measure the speed, pressure and temperature of the air at different heights. At that time, Col 'Buffalo Bill' Cody, too, was experimenting on similar lines for air-lifting men for military purposes. The colonel was a frequent visitor to Beverstone where they conducted joint experiments. It is said that some of the kites with delicate apparatus reached a height of about one mile. Occasionally, a kite broke away, trailing a long length of fine steel rope across the country. With the growth of Oxshott and traffic, kite flying became unsafe and difficult. William Dines, therefore, left Beverstone in 1906 for Oxfordshire to continue his upper atmosphere work. Using small balloons and instruments of his own design, heights of 10 miles were reached, providing him with invaluable data in hitherto unexplored fields. A wing of the Meteorological Office at Bracknell is named after William Dines in recognition of his pioneering work.

However, in Oxshott he is remembered for his regular Sunday attendance at St Mary's, Stoke D'Abernon. Punchard has recorded that, when the congregation left the church, 'to walk back the two miles to Oxshott, well ahead of the rest of us were three very tall men, Mr Dines and his two sons dressed in top hats and frocked coats who, because of their long legs, were soon out of sight across the first field'.

Mr Dines served as an overseer of the poor, an office that originated in the sixteenth century. Relief of the poor was the responsibility of the parish to which they belonged, financed by a levy on all parishioners. Administration was by overseers appointed annually by the Church.

In 1920 Miss Raven of Uplands obtained a lease of 21 years of Beverstone from Mr Dines which, after about a year, she sub-let to A. J. Smellie. Mr Smellie then negotiated a direct lease from Mr Dines.

Mr (now Sir) Greville Spratt bought the freehold of Beverstone from Mr Dines in 1959 and lived there for several years. He was called to the Bar in 1968 and is a Justice of the Peace. He was Chairman and director of several companies, Lord Lieutenant of the City in 1972, a Liveryman of the Worshipful Company of Ironmongers since 1977 and a life member of the Guild of Freemen and served on its Court from 1982 to 1990. He is a member of the Surrey Scout Council and a patron of the Surrey Charity Group. Since 1978 he has been Alderman for Castle Baynard Ward and was knighted in 1987 on becoming Lord Mayor of the City of London.

Sir Greville sold Beverstone to Derek Carver in 1971, who has lived there with his family since then.

One of the twelve wells which, if necessary, could have been reactivated to supply good quality drinking water to the village during the last war, is in the grounds of Beverstone.

Uplands was the mansion on the Leatherhead Road next to the Victoria Inn. It was built by Messrs H. G. & A. Osman Ltd in the first decade of the present century. Like other houses of that period, it too had large grounds totalling about 5½ acres and a lodge. The building, architecturally, was nondescript, but the gardens were lovely. There was also an orchard and a few of the apple trees still litter the pavement with windfalls.

The first owner of Uplands was a Mr Raven who lived there with his family. It is said that he and his wife died tragically in a car accident in 1920. Miss Raven then moved to Beverstone. It was the home of Mr and Mrs H. A. R. Russell during the Second World War and Frank Burton and his family in the 1970s.

During Mr Raven's time, Uplands was used as a children's school. It was also the venue of a gathering of the Birdshill Group on 2 April 1946 for Sir Adrian Boult's talk on music.

The mansion was demolished in the early 1980s and the site developed for housing in two stages. First was the building of seven

81

dwellings with an approach from a new road called Torland Drive off Birds Hill Drive, and then five houses from a drive off the Leatherhead Road.

Copsem Lane is the part of the main Oxshott-Esher road from the Sandy Lane junction to the Milbourne junction, Esher. At various times, it has been called Coplseham and Copsham and in 1945, it was Copsen Lane. At the turn of the present century, it was just a country lane with farmland and fields on either side reaching up to Queen's Drive. On the section between Round Hill and Sandy Lane, a number of attractive houses were erected between 1850 and 1860 on both sides of the road. Copesham House with a farm of the same name and Arbrook Farm on the opposite side are the oldest in this area. The present Copesham House was built about 1900 but has retained much of the older Copesham Cottage. There were stables with a chiming clock on which the farm workers and neighbours relied for accurate time. The farm had a dairy herd and delivered milk twice daily.

Copesham House was the country residence of Sir Herbert Cook up to 1927. His main residence was at Richmond, Surrey. Sir Herbert had a magnificent collection of old masters, some of which were in Copesham House.

Mr Blakey was Sir Herbert's head coachman and riding master to his children, and with his family lived in the Round Hill Cottage, now called West Winds. He lost his life in France in the First World War but his family continued to live in the cottage until the Copesham estate was sold in 1927. His daughter, Sybil Bradnam, has described life in Oxshott vividly during 1910-1927.

George Meredith lived in Copesham Cottage from 1857 to 1864 and some of his best works — *Richard Feverel, Evan Harrington* and *Modern Love* — were written there. Meredith did not own the cottage. A farm worker named Grange and his family lived in the cottage and Meredith lodged with them. His friend Swinburne often stayed with him and wrote the poem *Laus Veneris* there.

Gunters Mead and Rosemary Simmons Memorial Housing Assocation: Gunters Mead is one of the fourteen properties owned by a non-profit-making organisation called the Rosemary Simmons Memorial Housing Association. Roger Gunter Simmons and his wife Iris, then of Deep Furrows, Stokesheath Road, Oxshott, established the association in 1959 in memory of their daughter Rosemary, who was tragically killed in 1954 in a car accident at the tender age of eight. The sole object was to provide homes for local, independent, elderly persons of limited financial means in North West Surrey. A committee was formed with Mr Simmons as chairman to further and administer the project.

The first property acquired by the association was Alstonfield in Claremont Lane, Esher. It was converted into 20 self-contained units for letting at affordable rents. The scheme was so successful and demand so great that the association purchased and adapted other properties on similar lines.

Garden Court was the big house in Copsem Lane built in 1926 by Mr Kettle. It had extensive grounds with ornamental gardens laid out by Cheal's of Crawley, Sussex. With a change of ownership, the name was changed to Newington Court. George Dawson, post-war Army surplus dealer and importer of fish, lived there before it was acquired by the Trust. The name changed again to Gunters Mead when it was purchased by the Association in 1969. Forty one-bedroom flats were built in the grounds in 1970 with the first occupancy in 1971 and the house itself used for central facilities. Subsequently ten more flats were erected in the grounds and an old building converted. However, the big house has now been converted into fourteen flats for the active elderly and the communal facilities are housed in a new building called Garden Lodge.

Unlike Alstonfield and some other properties, residents in Gunters Mead purchase the leasehold of their flats, but the purchase price is refunded in full when they leave. In the meanwhile they pay a service charge to cover the cost of a resident manager and maintenance and upkeep of the buildings and gardens. John and Pauline Steer were the resident managers for 21 years, retiring in 1995.

The Association has traditionally catered for the elderly but, conscious of the lack of cheap housing in this part of Surrey, now provides housing for people of all ages.

Both Roger and Iris Simmons were awarded MBEs in 1975 for their interest in the welfare of the elderly and efforts to provide affordable homes for them. Regrettably Mr Simmons died before he could receive his award. His wife was then appointed chairman of the Association. She retired in June 1982 and was appointed Life President. She continues to take an active interest in the laudable work of the Association.

Gunters Mead was the setting for the latest Hercule Poirot TV series with David Suchet playing the leading role.

Queen's Drive is one of the four residential roads in Oxshott built over farmland. Heatherwold and Langley were the first two houses to be built soon after the road was made in 1898.

Heatherwold was the home of the Northcott family for about 35 years. They contributed generously to the Church Building Fund. Mr Northcott was chairman of the Oxshott Heath Conservators and president of the Oxshott Horticultural Society.

Mrs Alice Northcott was the first president of the Women's Institute, elected in 1919. She supported the British Red Cross Society and during the First World War, Heatherwold became the local 'workroom' for hospital supplies.

Heatherwold was subsequently occupied by a brother of the Greek shipping magnate, Mr Goulandris. The building is now called Queen Anne House. Planning consent for four new houses has been granted.

Langley was built for Mr and Mrs Humbert who supported the Church and the school, and helped to build social and recreational facilities. Their son was killed in France in the 1914-18 war.

Parklands: Two solicitors had bought the lease of the whole of one side of Queen's Drive and built Parklands where, much later, Lord Alfred Robens of Woldingham, first chairman of the National Coal Board, lived. Parklands is a country house in 6¼ acres of grounds with an ornamental rose garden, a woodland with a stream, stables and two staff cottages.

The Mount was built in 1905 as a honeymoon house for Mr and Mrs Piersse on land bought from the solicitors. The grounds then consisted of about eleven and a half acres laid out with the then customary tennis lawn, bowling green, croquet lawn, vegetable and formal gardens and woodlands. The formal ornamental gardens were designed by Cheal's of Crawley who had laid out gardens at Garden Court (Gunters Mead) and Hever Castle. One of their employees became Mr Piersse's gardener and worked for forty-four years, living in a cottage in the grounds. The cottage has been enlarged and is now called *Bearland*.

After Mrs Piersse's death in 1957, the property was empty for about a year and a developer wanted to build four houses there but Durham Wells, the then owner of Parklands, intervened and bought The Mount. Mr Wells retained the gardener's cottage and sold a plot with almost half the grounds of The Mount. *Coppers* was built there. The showpiece ornamental gardens were reduced to about five and a half acres, but Mr Wells' intervention prevented it from complete destruction.

Mr and Mrs Charlish bought The Mount in 1959 and brought up their three children there. After service with the RAFVR during the war, Ralph Charlish trained with Pan American Airways and started Compass Travel in London with £100 borrowed from a friend. He specialised in business travel and was so successful that he opened an office in Nigeria. He sold out in 1980 but remained chairman and managing director until his death in 1982. Ralph Charlish was the last man to be seen wearing a homburg waiting at the Oxshott Station for the London-bound train.

His widow, Catherine, continues to live at The Mount. She is a Fellow of the Institute of Travel and Tourism and still travels. She is a committee member of the Esher History Society and a qualified journalist.

Catherine Charlish sold some land and thereon was built the road called The Spinney. Three 'luxury' houses have been built there.

Their daughter Anne became a writer and editor and is the author of *A World of Horses* published in 1982. Son Jeremy was in the family travel business and is now manager of an air freight company at Norwich airport, and Judith, the other daughter, is a school teacher.

Heath House was built in 1899 for the philosopher, Bernard Bosanquet. He was a Fellow of the British Academy and was later appointed Professor of Moral Philosophy at the University of St Andrews.

Ranworth was built about 1910 on a central plot between Parklands and The Mount on land belonging to the solicitors. At one time, it was occupied by an elderly lady and then sold to Guy Salmon. Mr Salmon bought dilapidated properties and, after refurbishing, sold them on. Ranworth was the home of young Frost of the Battle of Arnhem.

Wood Dene was another large house which was requisitioned in the last war for the Canadians. After the war, attempts to sell were unsuccessful. Finally a developer bought it and new houses have been built.

In 1959 there were only nine houses in Queen's Drive, and now there are twenty-five and it is still expanding.

Fairoak Lane was originally a cart track called Steer Lane which went through Prince's Coverts and connected Warren Lane to the junction with the road to Chessington and Epsom. Steer Cottage and a smallholding of about four acres at the end of Broomfield Ride were part of Birds Hill Farm in 1777 and farmed by Abraham White.

Fairoak Lane may be connected with Gospel Oak or King's Tree which in 1815 stood on the boundary of Cobham close to the 'racecourse', marked on maps as Claygate Common. The oak was the boundary marked later by a Coal Tax post.

The Oxshott end of the cart track for approximately half a mile was improved about 1918 and the first houses built on both sides. In 1925, the whole road from Oxshott to Chessington crossroads was widened and asphalted when more houses were built along and around the first half. After the Second World War, Stokesheath Road was improved and new roads — Fairoak Close, Moles Hill and Parkfields — built for residential properties. Smaller houses with fairly large gardens were constructed.

Birds Hill Estate: Houses along Birds Hill Rise were built in the 1890s. At the beginning of the new century, the Commissioners for Crown Lands released more land for housing on the east side. Most of the original houses on Birds Hill Road, Birds Hill Drive and Princes Drive were built between 1914 and 1925. All the houses were on plots sufficiently large to have sizeable gardens, tennis courts and swimming pools. The next development in the area was Broomfield Ride, Spicers Field, Furze Field and Leys Road. The most recent developments are Montrose Gardens and Torland Drive. New houses continue to be built but basically they are infills on ground between houses. A number of beech hedges have given way to brick walls, changing the character of the estate.

Hill House in Birds Hill Drive was the home of G. G. Vertue until he died in 1917. Previously he lived at Knodishall in Copsem Lane. Knodishall is now called Avalon. He was the Hon Treasurer of the Church Building Fund and Hon Clerk to Oxshott Heath Conservators from 1904 until his death. He was also actively involved in Oxshott Men's Club. After Mr Vertue's death, Hill House was occupied by Mr and Mrs Guy Morrish until his death in 1920. His widow continued to live in Oxshott at Orchard Cottage until her death in 1934. Mrs Sybil Morrish was the Hon Secretary of Oxshott Women's Institute and President in 1930.

During the last war, it was the home of Archibald Nathan, who was the proprietor of Nathans Wigs in London, hiring out wigs, costumes and jewellery to the theatrical trade.

Oakshade Road and Red House: Oakshade Road started as a grass path through Hill Meadows to Oak Hill Farm which went down to Steels Lane. Oak Hill was a part of Oakshade Farm (previously called Oxshott Farm and later to be known as Danes Hill Farm) owned by the Eastwood brothers. The grass path over the years became a dirt track and in 1896 was widened and made into a road. It had no surface dressing and was rutted and potholed. Esher Urban District (now Elmbridge) Council took no notice of residents' complaints. The Council disowned responsibility until 1953 when some residents discovered that, according to the Council's records, it was still classified as a footpath. The Council was responsible for maintenance and bringing it up to full standards for vehicular traffic. Oakshade Road was properly made in 1955.

Soon after the opening of the old Oakshade Road in 1896, Mr Eastwoods built a few cottages, some of which have survived. Two of them are Bembridge and Shorwell, facing St Andrew's in Oakshade Road. They were the gardener's and chauffeur's cottages. Bembridge was originally called Beverley, but Stan Taylor changed the name when he came to live there.

Red House gets its name from the red bricks and tiles used in its construction. It was the first large house to be built in Oakshade Road for a rich widow, Adriana Cobbett, in 1897 on land owned by Eastwoods. The plot extended to Steels Lane on the north and was bounded by Eastwood's other land where Midgarth was built later and by properties of Basil Pym Ellis on the west and on the south. A restrictive covenant prohibited building of more than one dwelling house.

Adriana purchased more land from Eastwoods in 1903 to expand her grounds on the Steels Lane side, and in 1906 she bought land from Ellis to increase her frontage up to Potters' Croft in Oakshade Road. Ellis stipulated that no building whatsoever could be erected and that a row of fine trees on his land $37\frac{1}{2}$ feet from the road would be preserved. Alas, the trees are no longer there.

Walter Edgley, a solicitor, bought the Red House property in 1908. He also bought, at about the same time, the properties of the late Mr Ellis between Steels Lane and Oakshade Road, which included the piece of land gifted to the Church Authorities in 1904. Edgley sold parts in 1917 and 1919 and, after the restrictive convenants had been lifted, he sold the remaining lot including Red House in 1960 to May & May (Builders) Ltd of Dorking. Red House was then converted into three flats. In the late 1930s, a Miss Bradbury was living in Red House.

Knott Park Estate: Knott Park House was the home of the McAlpine family of the construction and house building industries. The house was built at the turn of the century in a parkland setting surrounded by gardens and orchards for Robert McAlpine. Appointed a baronet in 1918 for his war work, philanthropy and donations to charities, Sir Robert lived in Oxshott until the late 1920s and moved to Cobham Court in the Fairmile. He died on 3 November 1934 aged 87.

Sir Robert sold the property to Oxshott Development Company owned by Mr Weiss and Mr Lever. Development started in 1936 and a number of plots were sold for moderate sized houses, but everything came to a halt with the outbreak of war in 1939. The main development took place in the 1950s and the property was extended by about 23 acres lying south of the bridle path. Knott Park House was divided vertically into five.

McAlpines were entrusted with the demolition of the medieval London Bridge and stones were distributed among various members of the family. Some of the stones were received by Sir Malcolm McAlpine who was the occupier of Knott Park House at that time. He had them inlaid in one of the walls.

The estate consists of 68 houses. Well-known persons have lived there including Dame Moura Lympany, concert pianist, who lived at White Acre in the Chase in the 1950s. She shared the house with a pianist friend, Tony Laurie.

The Ridgeway: The development of this housing estate was started in 1918 by Col May and completed in the 1930s. The estate comprises medium-sized houses on plots of about one third of an acre. Jazz singer, Linda Lewis, lived in one.

Silverdale Avenue is a relatively recent development. Houses were built in the late 1950s on Hill Meadow, which was a part of Danes Hill grounds. They are smaller than those in the Ridgeway.

Charlwood was another large mansion in its own grounds with the usual stables and other offices. Canadians had the use of it during the last war and, after their departure, it housed the homeless. The mansion was demolished early in the 1950s and a housing estate of 53 dwellings developed in Charlwood Drive by Messrs Berg of Esher. The Australian pop singer, Ruby Murray, best remembered for her song *Softly*, lived in one of the houses in Charlwood Drive.

Council Houses: After the opening of the railway and up to 1914, most of the houses built were large with extensive grounds. A few of them had cottages, but there was a shortage of dwellings for outdoor employees and other workers. After the war, the Council built a group of houses to the design of Leonard Martin FRIBA. The design was identical to houses in Cobham, Mount Cottages in Old Common Road. Martin lived in Cobham and had designed the since demolished old Cobham Cottage Hospital as well as the school now called Reed's. He had also designed Burnt Stub at Chessington. He made his name with Henry Treadwell in designing elegant narrow frontage buildings, a typical example being No 7 Hanover Street, London.

Crown Cottages have replaced the original houses.

Houses along Sheath Lane were built which included a poor-house. Laneside Cottages were built soon after. More Council houses were erected in the 1930s on less desirable land along the railway line and Blundel Lane. When the Council estate was developed, Blundel Lane was extended from Steels Lane towards Cook's Crossing along the east side of the orchard of Little Heath Farmhouse. The footpath to St Mary's, Stoke D'Abernon was diverted to come out opposite Irene Road. More and more of Ayling's farmland was taken over for housing in the Kenilworth Avenue, Waverley Road and Webster Close area. Kenilworth Avenue was Drift Way, so called as cattle were driven from the farm to the fields. A part of it still remains at the back of Nos 18-64 in Waverley Road. Since then, there has been hardly any Council building.

Milk Wood and Headlong Hall in Stokesheath Road, just west of the railway line, were buit in 1955 with flat roofs, stock brick walls and deep white painted eaves to the design of Philip Powell and Hidalgo Moya. The single-storey buildings were stepped downhill facing north-west across a large rough field, became two-storeyed towards the downhill end of Headlong Hall and were linked by screen walls and a separate unit of two garages. The careful detailing and adjustment of stepped line gave a subtle impression of horizontal lines.

Buildings of interest

According to Nairn & Pevsner, the only buildings of any architectural interest in Oxshott are Robin Hill, Milk Wood, Headlong Hall and Wild Wood.

The name Milk Wood brings to mind Dylan Thomas' radio play of 1954. Headlong Hall has been demolished.

Wild Wood in Princes Drive, dating from 1959, was designed by Kenneth Wood ARIBA, who also designed the Oxshott Village Centre. Wild Wood is a T-shaped house with cedar boarding outside. It was designed as a small house in a Surrey copse for two keen ornithologists.

Kenneth Wood was a qualified engineer as well as an architect. His designs include Emmanuel Church, Tolworth and St Paul's Primary School at Kingston upon Thames.

Cavaliers Court in the Leatherhead Road is another architecturally interesting house and is said to be by Bartlett and Grey. Originally a run-down cottage, it was restored and enlarged in 1959 using old materials to give it the appearance of an old house. The house, with its wood-clad exterior and open plan, was arranged to let sunlight in at all times. The cost limit was £4,000.

Wychwood also in the Leatherhead Road was a gardener's cottage in Danes Court grounds where Fernhill is now. About 1870 it was called Meadow Cottage. It has been built upon and enlarged.

OPPOSITE ABOVE: Danes Hill Mansion, c1890.
BELOW: Arrival of HRH Princess Alexandra of Teck to
open Oxshott Village Fair and Fête on 26 June 1912.
ABOVE: The procession starts for the opening of the
Bandstand on 26 June 1912.

ABOVE: Bevendean Mansion, BELOW: and the staff in
1899.

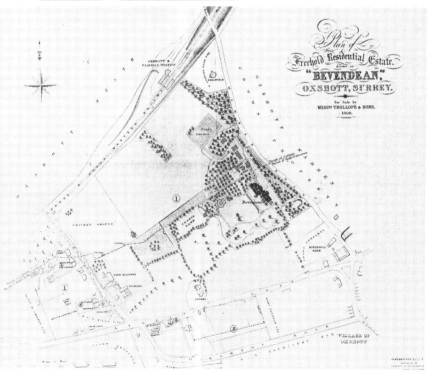

ABOVE: Basil Pym Ellis. BELOW: Plan of Bevendean
Residential Estate, 1908.

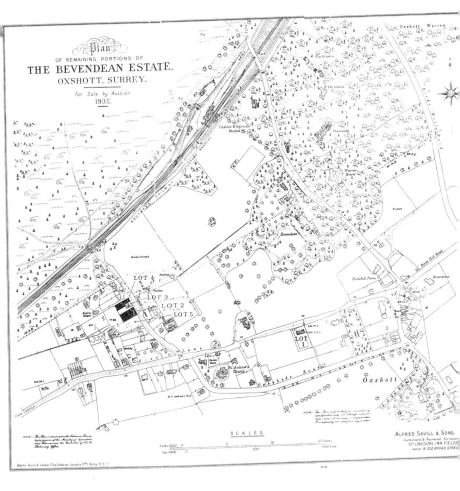

Sale Plan of Bevendean Estate, 1935.

94

ABOVE: Treetops. BELOW: Bevendean House in
Sheath Lane, with 'BPE' and '1894' inscribed on the front.

ABOVE: Englefield. BELOW: The Warren.

ABOVE: The Gables. BELOW: Pinewoods House.

ABOVE: Robin Hill. BELOW: Beverstone.

ABOVE: Mr Dines with instruments on the roof of
Beverstone. BELOW: Queens Drive, 1905.

ABOVE: Queens Drive, 1910 and BELOW: in 1996.

ABOVE: Steer Cottage in Steer Lane, c1890. BELOW:
Returning from Epsom, 1907.

ABOVE: St Andrew's Church (Temporary Building), 1905. BELOW: Opening of Oxshott Village Fair and Garden Fête, 22 June 1910, Mr H. Keswick speaking, Mrs Lambert presiding.

HOUSES OF THE LORD

Life in a village usually revolves around three essentials — pub, school and church, and no village is complete without all of them. Oxshott had pubs dating back to 1766, the school came along a half century later in 1818, and then there was a pause of 87 years before the village had its church and became complete. Oxshott had too few residents in the nineteenth century to afford a church. It was only after the arrival of the railway in 1885 and the building of large mansions thereafter that the population increased, but even then it was only 571 in 1901, (for the whole of the parish of Stoke D'Abernon of which Oxshott was a part).

St Marys' at Stoke was the parish church and people had to walk 1½ miles each way in fair and foul weather as not many had transport of any sort. The route to the church was a muddy track starting at the High Street junction with Steels Lane, through Little Heath (later known as Ayling's) Farm, across meadows and a swampy area. Canon Phillips had the track widened and gravelled to encourage villagers to attend Sunday services at St Mary's. The gravel path was often in a poor state of repair and the worst potholes were filled with all sorts of rubbish and rubble. The repairs were paid for from tolls collected at turnpikes.

With development and the increase in population, influential residents met informally to 'consider what steps can be taken towards providing a Chapel of Ease or Church at Oxshott'. They approached the Rector, Rev A. S. P. Blackburne, who wholeheartedly approved the idea, even though it would reduce the size of his congregation (and income) at St Mary's. He went out of his way to help. However, he advised them not to embark on too ambitious a scheme. He suggested a modest building which could serve as a temporary church to be replaced later with a more dignified permanent one.

St Andrew's (Temporary Building)
A public meeting, which the Rector chaired, was held on 24 May 1904 at the Royal Kent School. Basil Ellis offered to donate a site at the corner of Steels Lane and Oakshade Road (the present site). Frank Eastwood of Danes Hill, on his own and his three brothers' behalf, promised £250, provided that a definite start for a permanent church be made in the near future. The offer did not apply to a temporary building. After lengthy discussion, the meeting agreed unanimously that 'it was out of the question at the

time concerned to erect a permanent Church and that it would be wise to erect a temporary Church of iron and wood, or some other suitable material, on the site so kindly offered by Mr Basil Ellis, leaving it open for future consideration whether a permanent Church should be erected on that site or somewhere else'. A committee consisting of the following residents was appointed:

The Rector and Mrs A. S. P. Blackburne, Mr & Mrs B. A. Bristowe, Mr & Mrs Benson Clough, Mr & Mrs B. P. Ellis, Mr & Mrs L. C. Verrey, Miss Grey, Mrs Howell and Messrs R. Ashford Dash, W. R. Darrad, Grimshaw, Hasloch, Kirk, R. J. Lambert, J. J. Morrish, Neville Matthews, F. A. Phillips (the late Canon Phillips' son), Rudd, Skelton, G. Stoton and G. G. Vertue. Mr Vertue was appointed hon secretary and Mr Verrey, hon treasurer for the Church and Curate Funds.

A large committee by any reckoning, it seems that they were all dedicated as none of them missed any of the numerous meetings. The committee's deliberations led to a public meeting at the school on 24 June 1904, when the building of a temporary church costing between £400 and £500 was unanimously approved. Basil Ellis subscribed £75 (in addition to the land he had donated), Benson Clough £60, Sir John Aird Bt MP £50, J. J. Morrish and G. G. Vertue £35 each, and Rev A. S. P. Blackburne £30. Other donations brought the total to £274 for the building and £92 for the curate funds and within a month the figures had risen to £412 and £150 respectively. The Bishop of Winchester, in whose diocese Oxshott was, congratulated the Rector on his leadership and sent a donation. Also, the Crown (the Lords of His Majesty's Treasury), contributed £40.

Approval of the building plans for erecting a wood and rough cast structure with a seating capacity of about 180 was granted and the foundation stone laid in the first week of August 1904. The building was completed in three months and the temporary church consecrated on Monday, 21 November 1904 by the Bishop of Southampton.

Commenting on the speedy completion of the building, *The Village* (Stoke D'Abernon) *Church Magazine* of December 1904 wrote 'Where all have worked so well, it seems almost invidious to make special mention of individuals, but the work would never have been accomplished as speedily and well and so economically if Mr Basil Ellis, with his great experience, had not personally superintended the work and given constant supervision from the beginning. Mr Nesbitt, from Messrs Lucas, Aird & Co., practically acted as a voluntary clerk of the works, and Mr Andrews was always ready at hand to do innumerable odd jobs and was simply invaluable. Shortly before the day of dedication, Mr Basil Ellis transformed the ground into a garden with beautiful plants and shrubs. Mr Verrey also brought all his organising powers to bear and spent days in seeing after all the necessary details which are so apt to be overlooked. Mr Bailey also gave invaluable help in connection with the laying of paths and grounds. Of the special gifts, we naturally turn first to the altar, pulpit, lectern and priest's stall, presented by Mr and Mrs Phillips and family in memory of the late Canon and Mrs Phillips. We can only say that they are worthy of any permanent Church that we may build however beautiful. The altar makes in itself a link with the Mother Church, for it formerly found a place in the Chantry Chapel at Stoke. The pulpit is partly, at least, made of wood many hundred years old. The lectern is a copy of the one in Winchester College Chapel. Other gifts include a marble and alabaster font, presented by Mrs Benson Clough; a lectern, bible and prayer books for the priest's stall, from Major and Mrs Fullerton; a set of stoles for the use of the clergy from Mr Lambert; the bell, given by Sir John Aird, the organ by Mr and Mrs Basil Ellis; burse, veil and altar linen by Mrs Howell; gradine and altar covering from Mr G. G. Vertue'. The cost of building the temporary church excluding internal fittings was in the region of £400.

The organ was once an old cinema organ, a Mighty Wurlitzer, adapted for church use. It was replaced in 1960 by a new organ built by George Barlow. An electronic organ served as a substitute during the replacement work.

Holy services at the Royal Kent School then ceased which thereafter was used for childrens' education during daytime and for public meetings and recreational purposes in the evenings.

Fund raising activities such as concerts, musical events and plays, continued to meet the deficit in the buiding fund but so successful were the organisers — Ralf Morrish and his sister and the Verreys — that the fund was closed in June 1905.

Rev F. N. Skene was appointed curate in charge of Oxshott and took up residence in October 1906. He was previously for three years curate at St Mary's, Cowes with Rev A. H. McElwee. The latter, when located at Epsom, had officiated several times at Sunday evening services at the Royal Kent School, Oxshott. Rev Skene became the first vicar of St Andrew's, Oxshott. The church was usually filled to capacity for Sunday service. The offertories averaged £12 a month which were more than at St Mary's, Stoke D'Abernon. The collection covered general church expenses, including organist's fees, but the curate's stipends depended on annual subscriptions from parishioners which amounted to about £200 a year. There was no rent-free house for the curate.

The parish room was the front part of Oxshott Working Men's Club facing the church across the muddy path. It had cost £454 12s 2d (£454.61) in 1907.

The congregation kept pace with the increase in population. The temporary church could seat 180 but communicants on Easter Sunday 1909 were 182 and not everyone attending took Holy Communion. It became obvious that a larger church was required.

St Andrew's (Permanent Building)

The lead once again came from villagers. A public meeting under the chairmanship of the Rector, Rev A. S. P. Blackburne, was held on 25 May 1909 where a resolution proposed by R. Ashford Dash of Englefield, Warren Lane, and seconded by Trevor Castle of Wood Dene, Queens Drive, was unanimously passed 'that in the opinion of this meeting the time has arrived when steps should be taken with a view to early erection of a permanent Church of St Andrew, Oxshott'.

R. J. Lambert suggested a building costing not less than £5,000 and was strongly supported by James Northcott who stated that 'it would be an insult not only to themselves but to Almighty God to build a Church for what most of them would spend on their stables'. A general committee was appointed. Mrs Basil Ellis had sent £100 to kick-start the Church Building Fund.

The Rector, duty bound, reported to his superior, the Bishop of Winchester, Herbert E. Winton who, while agreeing with the idea of a permanent Church in Oxshott, replied 'Before any definite steps are taken, I should like to have the benefit of the opinion of several of the leading Church people in the parish, upon whose judgement I could rely, upon the important questions which are involved in this policy of the erection of a new Church. For this purpose, I am inviting a small commission to enquire into the matter and to report to me upon (a) the probable future development of the population in the neighbourhood and the district to be served by the new Church; (b) the suitability of the site of the present temporary Church as the site for a new Church; (c) the provision that must, before long, be made for a new burial place in the parish. Those whom I am inviting to serve upon this commission are the Rev A. S. P. Blackburne, Rector of Stoke D'Abernon; The Rev Prebendary Grane, Vicar of Cobham; R. A. Dash, Esq., Englefield, R. J. Lambert, Esq., Danes Hill, Oxshott; Trevor Castle, Esq., Wood Dene, Oxshott'.

Lengthy correspondence ensued. The Bishop wanted an assurance that the village would provide sufficient funds not only for the building but also its maintenance and other ancillary expenses, such as heating, lighting, cleaning, repairs, organist's salary. He also wished a capital fund for the vicar's salary. The Bishop envisaged a new parish of Oxshott after the Church had been built and consecrated.

106

It was agreed to build a new Church on the site donated by the late Basil Ellis and to establish a permanent endowment fund of £2,000, half of which would be raised by the villagers and the other half donated by the Ecclesiastical Commissioners for the incumbent's salary.

In the meanwhile, a number of sub-committees had been formed to deal with specific items such as raising money, endowment fund and building plans. People started sending donations. Some were impatient to see an early start but the hon treasurer, Mr Vertue, was against it and on 14 February 1910 wrote 'I hope this [to start building] will not be attempted until we have the necessary funds in hand. It is a bad principle to start with a debt, and I don't think any of us would agree to make ourselves responsible to the builder unless the whole money is in hand'.

A drive to collect money then started in earnest with the curate, Rev Skene, in his element organising and co-ordinating various activities. Letters appealing for money were sent to all residents. A fair and garden fête was organised on 22 June 1910 at Danes Hill. It was opened by Mrs Keswick, wife of H. Keswick MP, and raised £520. The band of HM the 7th Queen's Own Hussars under James Slattery provided music. A similar fête was held in the grounds of Lt Col & Mrs Bowen Buscarlet's Manor House, Stoke D'Abernon, which yielded £380. All the expenses were borne by the owners of the properties. Concerts, amateur theatricals, competitive sporting events were also held, but the village fête and bazaar was the main fund raiser and became an annual event. The fête held on 26 June 1912 in the grounds of Mr and Mrs Lambert's Danes Hill was opened by HRH the Princess Alexandra of Teck in the unavoidable absence of HRH the Duchess of Albany. It produced £716 for the Church Building Fund.

The committee had to grapple with some formidable and exasperating problems. The sudden death of Basil Ellis in 1907 was a great blow. At one of the meetings, it was suggested that the new Church 'should be erected for the Glory of God and in memory of the late Mr Basil Ellis'. Shortly afterwards villagers were upset to learn that the trustees of his estate had instructed Messrs Trollope & Sons to sell Bevendean by auction. Then came the news that Messrs Boniwell, a reputed firm of estate agents in Surbiton had sold Bevendean to Ernest Schiff to establish a Home of Recovery in memory of his late brother Alfred George. The report was unfounded, but nonetheless, caused such bitterness and unpleasant talk of betrayal that Mrs Ellis requested that her husband's name be not mentioned in connection with the proposed new Church as 'there seems to be much unkind feeling at Oxshott at the present time'. Her son-in-law, Trevor Castle, resigned as hon secretary of the Church Committee. Eventually matters settled down and both Mrs Ellis and Mr Castle actively supported the Committee.

Bureaucracy prevails everywhere and the Church is no exception. Malcolm R. Aird and Walter Edgley bought in 1908 from the trustees of the late Basil Ellis's estate, land in Steels Lane and Oakshade Road, subject to the gift of the plot donated to the Church. When the Church Authorities failed formally to accept the gift within five years, *ie* by 24 May 1909, it technically reverted to the buyers. When it was discovered that the Church Authorities had lost the title, Messrs Aird and Edgley waived their right so that building could proceed.

Messrs Caröe & Passmore, architects specialising in church buildings, were commissioned to design the new Church with a seating capacity of 500.

Caröe's original design for the proposed Church was ambitious and was estimated to cost £10,000, whereas the committee had expected to spend no more than half that. He was asked to review the plan, without altering the design, so that the Church could be enlarged as and when circumstances permitted. Caröe's revised plan provided a sanctuary, chancel, side chapel, vestries and two bays of the nave, and was estimated at about £4,000. He was authorised to invite tenders. Quotations received ranged between £5,000 and £6,500. The two lowest were from Messrs H. G. & A. Osman, local builders and Messs Cornish & Gaymer of North Walsham, Norfolk, and the difference between them was only a few pounds. After much discussion and breast beating, the contract was given to Cornish & Gaymer as they had worked with Caröe & Passmore on similar projects.

The foundation stone of the Church was laid by the Duchess of Albany on Ascension Day, 25 May 1911, before a large gathering of distinguished people including the Lord Lieutenant of the County, the Bishop of Winchester, the Rector of St Mary's and his curate in Oxshott, Rev F. N. Skene. The Bishop buried copies of the Parish (Stoke D'Abernon) *Church Magaziner, The Times, The Surrey Advertiser,* the *Churchwarden's Almanack,* the invitation card, the names of persons present, stamps, a gold sovereign, a crown, a half-crown, and a sixpence, behind the foundation stone for posterity. G. N. Abernethy fired a gun salute from his Broom Hall grounds.

The building was completed on schedule in spite of wet weather and a number of other problems such as a threatened rail strike in 1912 which would have delayed the delivery of roofing tiles. H. H. Boughton fetched them from Reading in a horse-drawn cart. The new Church was consecrated in the name of St Andrew on Saturday,

30 March 1912 by Rt Rev Herbert Edward Winton, Bishop of Winchester, in the presence of many church dignitaries and a large congregation. One hundred and eleven people took Holy Communion. The Duchess of Albany, accompanied by her Lady-in-Waiting and Captain E. Seymour, Comptroller of the Household, attended the Thanksgiving Service.

At that time, the Church Fund had £5,200 and was just able to meet the bill of £5,199 12s 9d (£5,199. 64p). The cost would have been appreciably higher but for the generosity of a number of residents. Mrs Basil Ellis paid for the Lady Chapel as a memorial to her late husband, Edgar Dudley defrayed the cost of filling the east windows with stained glass, the stained glass window for the north sanctuary was given by R. J. Lambert and the south transept window and two churchwardens' wands were the gift of W. E. Faulkner. Other gifts were the High Altar by Whitaker Ellis and a processional cross by J. R. Grimshaw. The processional cross was in use in 1914, although Janet Freeman mentions 'an excellent silver-gilt one, designed by Caröe in 1919, which later became an Altar Cross'. The beautiful white font of superb workmanship was given by Mrs Burgoyne of Malincourt, Oxshott.

St Andrew's, like many of the older buildings of Surrey and Sussex, is built in 'flint stone with a touch of half-timbering. Its free, late Gothic tracery is especially graceful. It lacks the hoped-for tower and longer nave'. Caröe's original plan, which the residents could not afford, provided that it could eventually become a five bay church with a gallery but, as actually built, it has only two nave arches and a temporary wall at the western end which gives it the fore-shortened shape.

A fine reredos designed by Caröe was erected in 1916 in memory of R. J. Lambert.

The stained glass east window designed by Oscar Patterson of Glasgow represents the Ascension and the chapel window the Crucifixion; the south transept window is Our Lord blessing little children and the excellent white windows in the Sanctuary are the work of Horace Wilkinson of London. The two memorial windows were dedicated and unveiled on Sunday, 1 December 1912. The Church has a seating capacity of 250.

With the establishment of St Andrew's, it was inevitable that the Parish of Stoke D''Abernon would be divided to give Oxshott its own Parish. This took place on 14 October 1913 when HM the King accepted the representations of the Ecclesiastical Commissioners that parts of the parishes of Stoke D'Abernon, Cobham and Claygate should be united to become the Consolidated Chapelry of St Andrew, Oxshott. The boundaries of the Parish were published in the *London Gazette* of 17 October 1913 and are shown on a wall map in the vestry of St Andrew's. The ecclesiastic parish of Oxshott was formally established on St Andrew's Day, 1 December 1913.

The patronage of the new Parish was surrendered to the Bishop of Winchester by the Rector of Stoke D'Abernon on 31 July 1913. Later it was transferred to the rural deanery of Leatherhead, archdeaconry of Dorking and diocese of Guildford.

Parish and parliamentary boundaries are not identical. Oxshott Polling District is separate from Stoke D'Abernon, although only one councillor represents both. Oxshott was in the Epsom parliamentary division of the County of Surrey but under the Surrey Review Order of 1933, it was included in the Urban District of Esher (Elmbridge).

The first wedding to be solemnised at St Andrew's was on Saturday, 19 April 1913, between Owen J. Humbert of Langleys, Queen's Drive and Miss J. A. Abernethy of Broom Hall. Sadly, the only son of the marriage, Captain Malcolm Humbert, was killed in World War II. A few weeks later on 7 June 1913, the marriage of his sister with Major C. E. Foxe-Male was blessed at St Andrew's.

J. J. Morrish of Danes Court gifted the site with the house in which the Vicar lived but died on 2 July 1919 before the formalities were completed. His family did not revoke the gift which the Ecclesiastical Commissioners accepted as a 'Benefaction in Suspense' of the value of £800. Then the Commissioners made a grant of £800 from their Common Fund.

The temporary church building of 1904 — not so temporary as it was in constant use until 1969 — became the Church Hall. Meetings of the Women's Institute were first held there but in 1914 a club room was added which St Andrew's acquired on 9 August 1963.

When St Andrew's was consecrated, there was not much money in the Curate's Fund. Fund raising continued unabated and £1,000 was handed over in 1913 to the Ecclesiastical Commissioners which they doubled and invested to produce a small annual income for the vicar. Efforts to raise money for the extension of the Church never ceased. By 1965 £15,000 had been collected which included £10,000 raised from the sale of the old school in the High Street.

The population of Oxshott had grown to 3,000 in 1961. It was considered desirable to extend the Church. Advice was sought from a local architect, Victor J. Syborn FRIBA, of Messrs George Baines and Syborn, London, who had built Birds Hill Croft (now Summerhill) at the top of Steels Lane as his residence. His design provided an extension at the west end side, including a gallery to give approximately 100 more seats in pews, enlargement of the vestry and accommodation for men and women of the choir. The

110

minimum estimated cost was £32,000; the scheme had to be shelved until at least £10,000 more had been raised. This was achieved by early 1969. By mid-1965, it was realised that building permission for the extension would be granted only if a car park was also provided. Finally it was decided to extend the Church on the west end side without a gallery. A vestibule and a new church hall were built and opened on 20 May 1971. It is hoped that one day the nave will be extended as originally proposed by Caröe.

The following have served as vicars of St Andrew's since its opening: Frederick N. Skene (1913-21), Nelson G. Davies (1921-38), Thomas C. J. Ford (1938-50), Herbert Evans (1950-66), Murray Hall (1967-72), John D. Green (1972-85), Bill Fillery (1986-90), Jeremy Cresswell (1990 to date). Rev R. S. Lound was the Priest-in-charge in the absence of the Vicar on war service overseas from 1942-45.

Baptist Chapel

The Chapel was the first established place of worship in Oxshott. It was built in 1873, thirty-one years before the temporary building of St Andrew's Church. The Chapel was off Sheath Lane at the back of four labourers' cottages, probably attached to Isaac Sheath's farm. The cottages were primitive, one-storey buildings with tarred roofs without ceilings and bare earth flooring and were erected before 1870. One of these cottages was occupied by Mr and Mrs Malthouse and was used as a meeting place by some of the Baptists. Mr Malthouse accompanied by George Boughton and Frederick John Kerry would walk on Sundays to the Chapel in Esher. With no public transport, going to Esher was not easy especially in winter. They wanted a local chapel and talked to other Baptists. All supported the idea and in particular the Bournes, Finches, Pullens, Simmons, Talbots and Whites were enthusiastic. However, there were difficulties. Most of the land in the village was Crown property and freeholds were almost non-existent. The only available freehold ground was a swampy patch known as 'Wapping Dock' off Sheath Lane not suitable for building, but there was a house on stilts. The site belonged to Miss Alice Grey who owned and occupied adjoining St Anne's Cottage. She probably gave the land for building the Chapel.

Miss Grey was active in the Church, Mothers' Union and the Women's Institute and served on their committees. She had built the neighbouring Pathway Cottage for a Miss Home who gave piano lessons. She also gave tea parties for the poor Eastenders of London who came by steam-engined trains at her expense. Invariably these

111

'poor' people ended up at the Victoria in the High Street in the evenings.

However, Mr Kerry, who had a grocery business in Hersham, was a man of great determination, energy and push. He had the land drained in 1868, solved various problems and had the Chapel built and in use in 1873. He transferred the legal ownership to the Trustees of the Esher Chapel in the following year for £15. The fire insurance cover on the Chapel premises was £100, fixtures, fittings, seating and books £50.

The first Minister was Mr Perrin who came from the Esher Chapel every Sunday. George Boughton was the first Deacon followed later by George Simmons. Music for hymns was provided by Miss Wadey and Miss Walden on a harmonium. The Chapel could accommodate about 50 persons and it was usually full.

The Chapel was so crowded that in 1935, the trustees were encouraged to purchase land in Steels Lane for £500 to build a larger one. However, the war came and the plan was shelved. During the war, attendances perforce went down and never recovered even after the war was over. The congregation continued to dwindle and the trustees were on the verge of closing it down early in the 1960s when Trevor Humber of Surbiton put new life in the Chapel. By his vigorous efforts, the attendance progressively increased to such an extent that in 1965 the local Baptists wanted to revive the Steels Lane project. Arthur Grimshaw of Waverley Road was appointed pastor in 1966. He wanted the new Chapel built quickly as the old one had no heating and toilets. He felt that a new building with modern facilities would provide great opportunities to expand, particularly the Sunday School. He was encouraged and supported by locals, but the Esher Chapel, which controlled the Oxshott Chapel, delayed matters. Attendance at the Chapel and at the school started declining and Mr Grimshaw resigned at the end of 1970. To continue his evangelical mission, he booked Oxshott Village Centre for 12 months at his own expense for Sunday services. His last service at the Chapel was at the end of December 1970 and the first at the Village Centre was a special Saturday meeting at the beginning of February 1971 with the London Crusader Choir under Reverend Doug Gray. The trustees then decided to close the Chapel and it remained empty for about three years.

Vernon Lane, of Pathway Cottage in Sheath Lane adjoining the Chapel site, bought it for £3,500 in 1973 to establish a Centre of Spiritualism and Faith Healing. He was himself a faith healer, and a leading member of the spiritualist church in Kingston and declared that the building would have broader objectives. The main

112

role of the Centre would be to help people to 'find themselves' and release stress and anxiety. Music and paintings would be used as preliminaries to relaxation for more fundamental work which would include clairvoyance and development of the sixth sense.

He had the old Chapel renovated, installed heating and toilets. The Centre started off well but there was inadequate support and Mr Lane closed it in 1986. He sold the Centre and Pathway Cottage in 1987 to B. D. Parmenter and Mrs J. C. Beckers. They converted the Centre to a private dwelling and have lived there since 1988.

Roman Catholic Chapel

The Catholic community had no place to worship in Oxshott and went to Esher, Leatherhead, Claygate or Cobham for Mass on Sundays. During the Second World War, twelve people held their first Mass in an office of Messrs Borax Consolidated Ltd who were located at Danes Hill mansion. When the company returned to London after the war, Danes Hill became a school. The Catholic group used one of the outbuildings as a chapel. Later the students' common room at Danes Court Domestic Science School was used on Sundays for services. Then the Catholic Church Authority acquired a site in Steels Lane in 1948 and erected a prefabricated building. It was called a Chapel of Ease but later renamed St Thomas of Canterbury. The Chapel came under the jurisdiction of the Church of the Sacred Heart, Cobham, and a priest came from there every Sunday to hear confessions and celebrate Mass. The first Mass was on 19 December 1949 and the celebrant was Father Gamble. Nuns from Cobham with local helpers prepared the Chapel on Saturdays for Mass on the following day. The Chapel was always crowded. During the week, Mrs Mary Nutcher of Crown Cottages, Steels Lane and others looked after the Chapel. It was popular and was also let for tea parties, old-time dancing and even bingo. Oxshott & Cobham Music Society held its concerts there.

In spite of its popularity and continuing demand for a local place of worship, the Chapel was closed on 27 October 1991. There has since been considerable concern and dissatisfaction.

The Cobham Church Authority obtained planning consent to develop the site with one building containing 10 one-bedroom units. The site with planning consent was then sold to Casablanca Properties Limited who have erected six cottage-style one-bedroom houses and a two-storey building providing four apartments of one bedroom each. The development is named Canterbury Mews and, unlike other recent developments, is aimed at 'first starters' and/or elderly retired people.

113

Henry Smith Charity

One of the greatest philanthropists of the sixteenth century was Henry Smith. He was born in Wandsworth, London, in 1549. The legend is that he was a homeless and penniless mendicant who, with his dog, begged his way through the county of Surrey and was flogged in Mitcham. He was then known as 'Dog Smith'.

However, Mr Smith became a silversmith and accumulated wealth. He was elected a member of the Worshipful Company of Salters and an alderman of the City of London Corporation. When he became a widower with no children, he set up a charitable trust for purchasing land for 'setting poor people awork' and for endowments to parishes in Surrey. The objects of the charity were to provide for (a) the poor, infirm or aged, (b) poor orphans, (c) families having more children born in wedlock than their labour could maintain and (d) poor people and their families if they work.

The Charity was prohibited from assisting (i) those who drank excessively, whoremongers, common swearers and pilferers, (ii) those who were notoriously scandalous, (iii) vagrants and (iv) those that had been incorrigible or disobedient to those whose servants they have been.

Almost every parish in Surrey has benefited from the Charity. Oxshott Mothers' Union received grants in 1900 and the following two years and again in 1911 towards expenses for meetings. Grants were also given to the Boot and Shoe Club whose secretary was George Stoton, the headmaster of the Royal Kent School. The Club was wound up in 1924.

W. Bishop and L. C. Verrey were among the trustees of the local branch of the Henry Smith Charity. Gordon Clark of Manor Cottage, Stoke D'Abernon, was another trustee. Alfred Williams of Willoughbys was secretary and treasurer in 1916. The Charity was, and still is managed by Cluttons, the estate agents in London, and Mr Bishop was in charge of it.

Henry Smith died in 1627 and was buried in Wandsworth Church.

Programme of Music, Oxshott Village Fair and Garden Fête.

Oxshott Village Fair
- and Garden Fete,
WEDNESDAY, JUNE 22nd, 1910.

PROGRAMME OF MUSIC
BY THE BAND OF
H.M. 7th QUEEN'S OWN HUSSARS
(By kind permission of Col. G. L. HOLDSWORTH),

Conductor ... Mr. JAMES SLATTERY.

2.15 P.M.

1 MARCH ... "Wellington" ... ... *Zehle*

2 OVERTURE "Maritana" ... *Wallace*

3 VALSE ..."The Druid's Prayer"... *Dawson*

4 SELECTION "The Dollar Princess"... *Leo Fall*

Introducing: Song, "Wiggle, Waggle, Waggle, Wooden Monkey"— Valse Lente—Duet, "Inspection"—Song, "Lady Fortune"—Valse Risoluto— Song, "My Dream of Love"—Trio, "Motoring"—Duet, "Ring of Roses"—"Typewriting" Duet—Quartet, "The Dollar Princess"—Valse Lente—Ensemble, "Chewska"—Trio, "America, Look Out."

5 HUNGARIAN DANCES 5 & 6 .. ... *Brahms*

6 HUMORESKE ... ... *Dvorak*

7 SCENES FROM "Carmen" ... ... *Bizet*

Poor Georges Bizet, Frenchman, wrote "Carmen" as his last opera, and because it did not achieve at once the success he had hoped, sickened of grief and shortly afterward died. Carmen is the hot-blooded, capricious Spanish coquette, who changes her loves with her clothes, now tantalizing Don Jose, the young military officer, now playing on the affections of Escamillo, the toreador; but in the end paying the penalty with her own life. In general the score is brilliantly piquant; in specifico it has numerous melodies so unlike any others that one does not soon forget them. World-famed is the Toreador Song, simply brimming with vigour and animation.

8 PATROL "The Wee MacGreegor" ... *Amers*

9 SUITE ... "Bohemian" ... ... *Hume*

1. The Appeal. 2. The Caravan. 3. The Tarentella.

10 LIED ... "Ivresse D'Amour" ... *Kappeller*

11 FANTASIA on Student's Songs ... *Douglas*

Synopsis:—Dulce Domun—A Roving—My Bonnie—Ten thousand miles away—Here's to a Maiden—A Tarpaulin Jacket—Who Killed Cock Robin—Upidee—There is a Tavern in the Town—Rosalie— Kemo, Kimo—Good Night, Ladies—The Golden Vanity—and "Here's a Health unto His Majesty" a la Tschaikowsky.

12 SELECTION of Harry Lauder's Songs ... *Hume*

GOD SAVE THE KING.

PRICE ONE PENNY.

ABOVE: Oxshott Village Fair and Garden Fête, 22 June 1910. BELOW: The ceremonial procession to lay the foundation stone of the permanent building of St Andrew's, Rev Skene leading the Duchess of Albany and Capt E. Seymour.

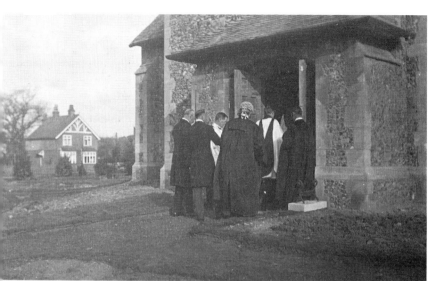

ABOVE: Consecration of BELOW: St Andrew's Church (1912).

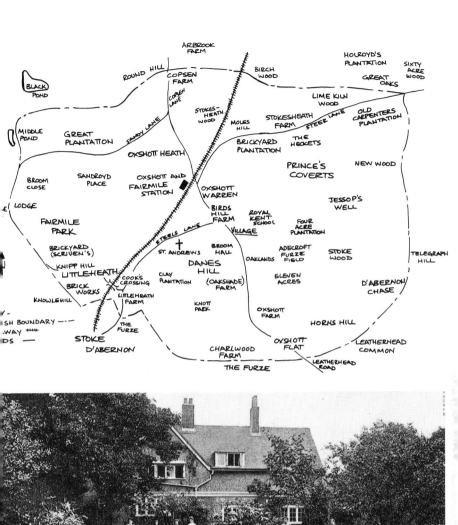

OPPOSITE ABOVE: Baptist Chapel with (left to right)
Frederick Kerry, Malthouse and George Boughton.
BELOW: Interior St Andrew's Church, 1915. ABOVE:
Boundary Map of the Oxshott Parish, 1913. BELOW: St
Ann's Cottage, Sheath Lane, c1860.

119

Farley's later Steels Lane, where the Doctor's messages
were left.

In Sickness & in Health

Oxshott did not have a resident medical practitioner until the beginning of the current century. Since there was no public transport, people had to walk to Esher to get medical attention. In case of an emergency, the doctor came on a push-bike. Later Dr Kitchen from Stoke D'Abernon came by horse. He arranged for people to leave messages at the Clock House in Steels Lane.

Dr T. C. Blackwell was the first resident doctor. He was a brother of the Blackwell of Crosse & Blackwell, tinned food manufacturers. Dr Blackwell lived at Oxshott Lodge and had his surgery there. He made his rounds in a chauffeur-driven car. The chauffeur, George Simmons, lived in Wells Cottage, which in those days was an outbuilding of Oxshott Lodge. George Simmons's son, Alan, is the local plumber living in Steels Lane.

As the village and its population grew, so did the workload. Dr Blackwell looked for a partner and found Dr Berridge. There was no suitable housing for the new doctor, who had to lodge and practise from one of the Crown Cottages in Steels Lane until his house was built in Birds Hill Drive. Dr Berridge was a commanding figure. His hobby was breeding Labrador gun-dogs. Later on he was appointed the doctor in attendance at all horse races held at Epsom, Sandown and Kempton Park.

After Dr Blackwell's retirement, Dr Watt joined Dr Berridge but he did not stay long. Then came Dr Lytle in 1948, walking from the station on a wet and windy morning to persuade Dr Berridge to take him on. Dr Lytle succeeded but little did he know that it would be easier to get a partnership and plenty of work in Oxshott than to find a house for his wife and young children. There were none to let and those for sale were much too pricey. He was advised to build one, but building land in a farming village was difficult to find. Dr Lytle approached Mrs Mollie Skinner of Englefield, Warren Lane, to sell him part of her vegetable garden in Holtwood Road. She turned him down flat but, on learning that he was a medical man who would live and practise from the house, she not only changed her mind, but also waived the usual transfer fee of £200.

So Dr Lytle built his house, where he lived and practised for 37 years, till his retirement in 1985. He had a largish garden which was looked after by a young seventy-year-old, Bert Kelleway. Bert had trained and worked at Queen Victoria's Osborne House on the Isle of Wight. Villagers made a presentation to Dr Lytle on his retirement, and he subsequently moved to Heath Ridge Green, Cobham, within the Parish of Oxshott.

A 'luxury' house has been built in a part of Dr Lytle's old garden in Holtwood Road.

To meet the needs of ever-increasing population, Dr Richard Glover was taken into partnership in 1958. He lived and practised from his home at Spinney Croft, Leatherhead Road. After Dr Berridge's death, Dr Glover was appointed the doctor for the three race courses. He retired from general practice in 1989 but has continued as doctor in attendance at the races. He sold his property in the Leatherhead Road and moved to Knott Park. The house was demolished and five 'luxury' houses were built on the site.

Dr Raphael came to Oxshott in 1964 and set up a surgery at her home, Windfalls, in Princes Drive. Although initially she practised within the National Health Service, she did not join the existing partnership. Like many other towns and villages, Oxshott was diffident about lady doctors. Dr Raphael concentrated on private practice.

Dr McKenzie came into the partnership in 1977 when Dr Berridge retired. He did not want to live in Oxshott, so left after one year. Dr Best replaced him, but he too was not resident in Oxshott. The partnership had in the meanwhile decided that it would be sensible to see all patients in one place. They arranged to have a wing added to the Village Centre in 1985 with rooms for Dr Best and Dr Down, who had joined the partnership that year. Dr Glover continued to practise from Spinney Croft. Dr Best left in 1989. The wing was extended in 1989 and now has rooms for three doctors, reception, waiting and ancillary services and a special clinic for children. The partnership now consists of Drs N. A. C. Down, R. J. Draper and Jacqueline Pickin.

Oxshott has been fortunate in its doctors, especially Dr Lytle, who has been involved in community welfare, and set up a fund to assist the needy when sick.

The Oxshott & District Medical Fund started with the retirement of local policeman, Robert Jenner, in 1970 after several years' service. Jenner was an old-fashioned, caring bobby for whom Dr Lytle organised a collection, which raised £780. Sir Robert Mark, the then Metropolitan Police Commissioner, who lived in Silverdale Avenue, made the presentation.

After the presentation the money still kept coming and soon totalled another £450. It was decided that this money could be the starting point of a permanent fund. A charitable trust called the Oxshott & District Medical Fund was established in May 1970 with the declared purposes of alleviating hardship, suffering or distress of needy residents during sickness or disability, by making grants of money or paying for services and facilities, including the purchase of special equipment for institutions and organisations. The first trustees were Dr John Lytle, Gordon Budd, Charles Slade and John Streeter.

Oxshott Christmas Fair helped with grants for the first two years and, after a lapse of 22 years, made another donation following the Fair in November 1994. People contributed by convenant but sadly not in recent years. Occasionally the fund has benefited from a death when the survivors have requested 'Donations to Oxshott and District Medical Fund' in lieu of flowers. However, its income has dwindled though it continues to fulfil its objectives.

The Fund has helped several people and donated equipment such as foetal monitors, 24 hour tape-electrocardiography, fibre-optic for chests and abdomen, audio-test machine, ice machine (physiotherapy), electric traction machine (physiotherapy), nebulisers, to the Cobham Cottage (now demolished and rebuilt) and Epsom General Hospitals, and to the Oxshott and Cobham Medical Practices. On behalf of the Fund, Dr Lytle presented a cheque for £2,000 in August 1994 to the Cobham Hospital Building Fund. It had already donated £1,000 in previous years.

Councillor Nigel Stevens is the hon treasurer.

The War Memorial.

IN WHICH WE SERVE

Residents of Oxshott are peaceable people, but they were in the forefront when war came. Many of them volunteered long before their call-up. There were no conscientious objectors. Brave and courageous people fought in the Boer War of 1889-1904 and in both World Wars. The following made the supreme sacrifice in those two wars:

1914-18

Major H. G. Gibson, Lt G. R. C. Child, Lt S. Harding, Lt E. G. J. Humbert, W. A. Ackerman, J. Auger, S. Bourne, A. Burgess, R. Carter, F. Coombs, F. G. Cotterell, E. Godfree, Cpl F. V. Finch, L. J. G. Finch, LCpl A. H. Foster, A. Harris, F. W. Parker, A. M. Rimer, W. Scarff, H. W. Selby, F. Skelton, E. P. Vickery and L. E. Wiles.

1939-45

E. E. Addis, E. A. Arliss, R. Stobi Akey, E. A. Comber, T. Creswick, J. F. Doelburg, H. G. Eady, I. K. Geddes, G. N. Gill, J. I. Green, B. C. Hart, C. Hatch, W. J. S. Hutcheson, P. C. Kelleway, B. E. Knight, J. F. Lee, P. Matthews, H. Northcott, C. S. M. Pearson, J. Pinches, R. H. Roxburgh, A. L. A. Tasker, J. Taylor, J. N. Todd, R. Wadey, J. Wilson and C. A. C. Young.

Their names are engraved on the War Memorial on top of Oxshott Heath and their courage, bravery and sacrifice remains undimmed. The stone memorial is a tall Celtic cross on a stepped plinth. It is not the original memorial, which was taller, but blown away in a gale. Scouts and Guides mounted guards of honour at both dedication ceremonies. Each year on Remembrance Sunday, the names are read out at a crowded service in St Andrew's Church, Oxshott, followed by a wreath-laying ceremony at the memorial. These are laid by the local branch of the Royal British Legion, the local Council, Oxshott Men's Group and Oxshott Scouts and Guides.

In World War II, 182 Victoria Crosses were awarded and Oxshott was associated with two. One was an outright posthumous award to Pilot Officer Cyril J. Barton RAFVR, for his bravery and gallantry in the raid on Nuremberg on 20 March 1944 when, after being hit, he rammed a German fighter, steered his plane away from residential areas and enabled his crew to bale out. His name is not recorded on the Memorial as he was not a resident of Oxshott at that time, but had been a Cub when living at Bevendean Laundry in Steels Lane.

The other VC was a 'collective' one. A special provision of the Royal Warrants allows the VC to be awarded to a selected officer or man in recognition not only of his own bravery but also that of his comrades. The posthumous VC awarded to Able Seaman W. A. Savage RN, who was a Volunteer Reservist in one of the fleet of motor launches in the Combined Operations raid on the Nazi battleship dock at St Nazaire on 27 March 1942, was not only to himself but also for the valour shown by many others in small boats of coastal forces. John May of Danes Close was First Lt on Motor Launch 446 in that raid. A force of 611 was involved of which 169 did not return. No fewer that five VCs were awarded to St Nazaire which was, in the words of Lord Mountbatten, Chief of Combined Operations, 'by far the highest proportion of VCs ever awarded for a single operation; and this is the measure of heroism of all who took part in that magnificent enterprise'. Winston Churchill described the raid as 'a deed of glory intimately involved in high strategy . . . The entire naval situation throughout the world was altered'.

Mr May is a modest and retiring man who seldom speaks of his wartime adventure and many who come in contact with him are totally unaware of his bravery.

Another courageous and brave man was Jack Frost of Ranworth, Queens Drive. He was one of the junior officers involved in the disastrous battle of Arnhem and had to take command when all his senior officers were killed. He was only 24 years old but, like a true professional, with cool calm and courage, he led back the few who survived. Frost had a long and distinguished career, rising to the rank of Brigadier in command of the Parachute Regiment. He died in 1994.

Among the survivors in the First World War was Jock Wyatt, the sweeper at the railway (Cook's) crossing. He was awarded the Military Medal for bravery. He had been wounded but carried on fighting. A bullet had lodged in his leg which could not be extracted without amputation. He would not hear of it and suffered pain and discomfort for years. When it became intolerable, he was persuaded by Dr Lytle to undergo surgery and had a wooden leg fitted.

Another Military Medal went to Sgt Gill of Irene Road, Oxshott, for courage and bravery.

Henry Wren was another war victim who had to live with his wounds, pain and discomfort until death. In spite of his disability, he volunteered to serve in the Second World War, but was turned down. Then he became a full-time Air Raid Warden.

Arthur Brown's application to join the forces was declined but he was appointed Recruitment Officer at Leatherhead.

Civilians did their duty too. They drove ambulances, became Air Raid Wardens, joined the Home Guard (Dad's Army) and the Fire Guard. The local unit of the Home Guard had its headquarters at Hill House, Archibald Nathan's home in Birds Hill Drive. There was a supplies depôt in Oxshott and Alfred Williams of Willoughbys, Leatherhead Road, was its hon treasurer.

Women, too, contributed to the war effort — growing foods, knitting, sewing and sending parcels of woollens and food to prisoners-of-war through the Red Cross. During the First World War, Mrs Northcott was active with the Red Cross and the Northcotts' home at Heatherwold, Queens Drive, was the war workroom to supply hospital requisites. A sewing workshop was organised in the 1939-45 war by Lady Morrell at Greenways, Copsem Lane. Mrs Verrey and her three daughters of The Warren, Warren Lane, helped nursing associations.

There were several air raid shelters, one on the green facing the school in the High Street. Each time the sirens sounded, children rushed across the road to the shelter. Other shelters were on the corner of Dr Lytle's old house at the junction of Steels Lane and Holtwood Road, at the top of Goldrings Road and at Broom's Corner.

Oxshott expected and did not escape air raids, as bonfires and beacons were lit in Prince's Covert to decoy German bombers away from London. Several air raids affected Oxshott during the last war but, due to the nature of the area, most of the bombs fell on waste land. One fell where Princes Drive is now, causing a huge crater and another landed in fields of Ayling Farm (now Waverley Road), but one came down in Steels Lane on 1 April 1944, demolishing Nos 1 and 2 Little Heath Farm Cottages. Both cottages were occupied by two unrelated families named Jones. Mercifully there were no fatalities or serious injuries. Edward and Gladys at No 2, with their two children, were blasted out and landed upon the roof of their demolished house, with Gladys nursing a broken arm. The occupants of No 1 were equally lucky and Mr Jones was found in his pyjamas wandering about in the garden. Surprisingly, his greenhouse was not damaged and is now a shed in a garden at Canada Road, Cobham. Both families were moved to the Schiff Recovery Home. A collection was made and each received £200. The two cottages were rebuilt. Mrs Gladys Jones now has a cottage in Arnewood Close.

Gaydon, the house nearby, had to be demolished. On the insistence of its owner, Orlando Hussey, it was rebuilt brick by brick from recovered materials.

Jock Wyatt swept the level crossing — he won the Military Medal in World War I.

Mr Hussey, nicknamed Banjo, was an engineer and the proprietor of Gaydon Motor Works in the Nissen hut in a yard at the back of the two shops now occupied by newsagent Everest and Osmans Cycles. Mr Hussey repaired anything and everything: bicycles, motorcycles, motor cars. However, the title was a misnomer.

Canadians were encamped at the brickworks during both wars and trained on Oxshott Heath. In the Second World War large mansions, such as Charlwood House, Old Farm House, Oxshott Lodge and Broom Hall were requisitioned to house commissioned and non-commissioned officers. After the war, some of the mansions were taken over by the local Council to house homeless families, with one room per family, common cooking facilities in corridors and shared bathrooms and toilets.

Whenever there was a call for help, Oxshott responded promptly and generously. In 1943, Oxshott, the smallest part of Esher Urban Borough District, was asked to raise £70,000 for the 'Wings for Victory Fund'. The village collected £84,215 or £50 per head of population. A year later Oxshott contributed £127,847, nearly £75 per head, to the 'Salute the Soldier Fund', against its set target of £70,000.

THE VILLAGE CENTRE

The Village Centre is Oxshott's tribute to the men and women killed in World War II but it nearly did not happen.

Although weary of war with its blackouts, doodle-bugs, chaotic transport and meagre rations, Oxshott managed to keep up its spirits. People met in small groups in each other's houses for cultural, intellectual and social relaxation. But war was never far away from their thoughts and one of the subjects often discussed was how best to express Oxshott's pride and gratitude to those serving in the armed forces, and those in the Civil Defence Services and allied activities. The 'Salute the Soldier' fund was a national effort but a need was perceived for a permanent memorial in Oxshott.

The Scott Committee's Report published in 1942 said 'We are convinced that the cardinal problem is how to re-focus cultural life within the village itself. For the women, the Women's Institute have shown in recent years how much can be done in this direction; more recently it has been seen that the Home Guard has provided a new common meeting ground for men . . . In many villages athletic clubs, musical and dramatic societies continue to function, but often are hampered by lack of a central meeting place. The team spirit engendered by village games makes for team spirit in the village as a whole. The question of village institutions is a fundamental one in the life of rural Britain . . . Every village should have what, for lack of a better name, may be called a community or social centre'.

Inspired by the report, two prominent residents, Geoffrey Metson of Danes Close and Leonard Thorpe of The Ridgeway held informal talks with residents representing various interests and found unanimity in favour of a community centre.

A public meeting on Saturday, 13 May 1944, attended by well over 100 residents, under the chairmanship of Neville Matthews of Birds Oak decided to establish the Oxshott Trust Fund. Two serving men on leave, John May of Danes Close and Stanley Taylor of Oakshade Road, observed that people in whose name money was collected, would have no opportunity to say how it should be spent. They wanted the decision deferred, but the meeting went on to agree:

'1. That an Oxshott Trust Fund be established for the purpose of collecting and investing funds to be used for the promotion of social, recreational and cultural activities for the benefit of the inhabitants of Oxshott and its immediate vicinity, without distinction of sex, or political, religious or other opinions.

'2. That the Oxshott Trust Fund be administered by a Management Committee of five persons to be appointed today with power to co-opt up to three other persons, such committee to be elected annually at the Annual Public General Meeting to be held in May until one year after the cessation of hostilities with Germany; thereafter a Public Meeting shall be convened to review the constitution of and the method of appointing the Management Committee. Further, that the Management Committee of five persons appointed today shall act as trustees of the Oxshott Trust Fund until such time as it is convenient to appoint the Official Trustee under the Charity Commissioners.

'3. That the Management Committee be empowered to settle the terms of the Trust Deed and to take such other steps as are necessary for implementing the decisions taken today.

'4. That the Oxshott Trust Fund should be used for the founding of a village centre for social, recreational and cultural activities.'

The meeting then elected a Committee of Management and Trustees: F. Neville Matthews (Chairman), J. T. O'Brien, JP*, Stella Proctor*, Leonard Thorpe*, Maude Wallaker*, and co-opted Wm T Bishop, Geoffrey Metson and Jack Woollcombe, and appointed Geoffrey Metson Hon Secretary and Solicitor and Leonard Thorpe Hon Treasurer. (* Trustees)

What would be included in the village centre would be decided after those in the services had expressed their views. Subsequently, Messrs May and Taylor joined the committee and, after discussing many other possible uses, it was agreed that a village centre would be the best memorial.

The Oxshott Trust Fund had a flying start and was enthusiastically supported. Within a year, individual subscriptions amounted to £1,357. From 1945, the Fund also benefited from a half-share of profits from the annual fête and horticultural show, and by 1955, it has £5,800.

Meanwhile, the Site Sub-Committee which included William T. Bishop, a leading figure in estate-management, was searching for a suitable location. Its first idea was to link with the Oxshott Village Sports Club and build the Centre on the sports grounds, in conjunction with its pavilion, but this proved impractical. After looking at alternatives, the two acre plot at the corner of Holtwood Road and Steels Lane was chosen. It had once been Isaac Sheath's field. The Crown Commissioners agreed to grant an option for a lease and preliminary building designs were commissioned. However, the money in the Fund was insufficient. Local and central authorities were approached for a grant. They were sympathetic, accepted the need but, in view of the national economy, could not promise early payment. Furthermore, there were restrictions on buildings, and materials were unobtainable without a licence.

Years went by. There were talks and more talks about location, plans, money, but not a brick was laid. People were asking not 'when' but 'if ever' the Centre would be built. There was talk about winding up the Trust and distributing the money among other causes. Neville Matthews, chairman of the Trust, resigned to enable him to propose a resolution at the Annual General Meeting on 16 November 1955 to abandon the scheme. It was passed by 175 to 66 votes. However, many villagers were bitterly disappointed and more so as Claygate had built their own Village Centre.

William Bishop was appointed chairman of the Trustees to wind up the Fund. Over the following four years, he explored various alternatives and worked hard to revive the original project. He resigned chairmanship in 1959 but continued as a trustee. The matter came to a head when the trustees were asked to exercise or renounce the option on the Holtwood Road site, as the Crown Commissioners could not keep it open. By then, Raymond (Remy) Ades had succeeded Mr Bishop in the Chair. He wanted the Centre built and was convinced that, even without any official help, grants or subsidies, sufficient money could be raised. He persuaded the trustees on 6 November 1959 to proceed with the scheme.

Remy Ades wasted no time. Assisted by his wife, Sally, he set out to make the project a reality. Their home, The Gables in Warren Lane, became the nerve centre for public appeals, door-to-door collections and other fund-raising events. Sufficient money was collected within a year to commission architect Kenneth Wood to design the building in such a way that it could be easily expanded. The foundation stone was laid by Lady Harris on 29 July 1961 and the building completed in a year. The official opening ceremony was performed on 8 September 1962 by Christopher Chataway MP, the then Parliamentary Secretary at the Ministry of Education.

Since then the building has been enlarged; first a bay was added to the main hall and then in 1985 a side extension for the Oxshott Medical Practice. Later the extension was enlarged to accommodate increased medical facilities.

Some grants or subsidies were received from local and national authorities; most of the money was contributed by villagers. The Centre exists largely because of Remy Ades' efforts. He was the chairman for over 30 years. Since his death, the Centre has been administered by a Management Committee, chaired by Eric Morgan of Princess Drive, and manned by volunteers. It is a non-profit making service to the community. The Village Centre is a worthy memorial to the war dead, and a proud achievement of the village.

ABOVE: Oxshott Village Centre. BELOW: Knowle Hill
Park (later Schiff's Home of Recovery).

THE BRICKMAKERS

Little Heath Brickworks were founded by John Early Cook Jr. He owned and lived at Knowle Hill Park which, after his death, became the Schiff Home of Recovery. He was a small, round-faced man with the voice of a sergeant major who looked upon his employees as his children, caring for them in both health and sickness — a most unusual employer. He spoke of them as 'being on his books' which entitled them to a free doctor, a ton of coal and at Christmas a goose and a bottle of brandy; also a present when there was a birth in their family. They had the job for life, but 'Woe to any man who was knocked off the books' for misbehaviour, for he was seldom taken back. Perhaps Beveridge adopted Cook's ideas, refined and enlarged them for our social security system.

John Early Cook was born on 9 May 1823 in a tenth century house at Nunsbury, Hertfordshire, and inherited at the age of 13, a vast estate there as well as a large number of tenements in Clerkenwell and the Minories in London. He went on to read mathematics at Brazenose College, Oxford where, after getting a double first, he stayed on for a further two years for an MA degree in 1847. Then to complete his education, he spent two years travelling in southern Europe, Egypt and India and made a special study of the layout of large estates. He returned to his birthplace and took up the reins of managing his properties, but his ambition was to establish an estate where 'master and men, mistresses and maid servants' could live and work together in peace and harmony. He achieved this when in 1855 he settled in Cobham, chosen because it was within easy reach of London — just an hour's drive in his 'coach and two', cheapness of land at £10 an acre and the suitability of the soil for growing exotic shrubs and trees. It could well be that he knew Cobham well as his first wife, Mary Jane, daughter of Rev Alfred Burmester, came from Mickleham. His second wife was Elizabeth, daughter of Patrick Ogilvie of the Indian Army, who outlived him. Neither bore him a child and that was his great disappointment. He bought a 50 acre site and built a large, attractive mansion on high ground with stables, cowsheds, vegetable garden and servants' cottages well out of sight behind trees and shrubs. It took him over a decade to lay out the gardens and park with its beautiful, rare and specimen plants, shrubs and trees, and an orchard.

Knowle Hill Park estate was self-contained in all respects except for a farrier. Frank Holden, a blacksmith of Cobham with his forge where Pennys, the ironmongers shop now is, was the only outsider employed — to shod Cook's horses. Mr Abbot was Cook's agent, Mr Preston the coachman, Mr Welch the gardener, Mr Buckle the herdsman and Mr Farrow the carpenter. They all lived on the estate or the nearby brickyard.

Cook was fond of horses and dogs. He could expertly handle a 'coach and two' and was often seen driving his 'dog cart' in the village. He was particularly proud of his horses as each of them had been fathered by the Derby winner Blair Athol. He had a great sense of humour and wanted his employees to be joyous and see the funny side of things. It is recorded that Cook subjected candidates to various tests which included one for humour. For example, before appointing Preston, an ex-serviceman, as head coachman, Cook asked him to stand with his back to the wall in the 'stand at ease' position. Then Cook in his sergeant major's voice barked out 'Attention; about turn', which Preston did but, when the third command was 'Quick march', realising the impossibility, he started laughing. Cook gave him the job.

Cook started a school in an iron hut in his brickyard for toddlers too young to walk to Oxshott or Cobham. Miss M. M. Lock was the first teacher there and, when she left to marry Arthur Brown Jr, the foreman at the brickyard, Miss Kate Ayling succeeded her at an annual salary of £25. The hut was used in the afternoons by local women as a meeting hall for sewing, knitting and social activities.

He never missed the Sunday service at St Mary's and attended Sunday afternoon service at the school, where he chose the hymns and read the lessons.

Cook's business activities in London led him to join the Worshipful Company of Carpenters in 1844. He was elected Master in 1885. His father (John Early) had achieved the same distinction in 1826. Portraits of both father and son can be seen in Carpenters Hall.

When Knowle Hill Park was completed, Cook cast about for something else to do. He realised there was money to be made from bricks. There were small brickfields at Claygate and Hatchford. Probably there was a brickfield at or near Brickyard Plantation in Prince's Coverts, for Katherine Edsau (Edser) 'of the Brickhouse' was buried in Oxshott in 1625. Also maps show brick kilns in the Brickyard Plantation. He purchased 30 acres adjacent to Little Heath and set up the Little Heath Brick Works with eight kilns. All the building work, digging out clay, carting sand, moulding bricks, drying and firing was carried out manually. The average daily output per man was 1,000 bricks and, when required, reached 1,500. The bricks were of top quality and were used to 'build' Oxshott and later also in 'Oxshott Fireplaces' exhibited at the Ideal Home Exhibition in the 1950s.

There were plans in the 1870s to build a railway line to Guildford which would have been near his house. Cook strongly opposed the project but, in 1883, struck a deal to sell 2½ acres of his brickfield to the Railway Company for £1,012 with a side line to the brickworks free of charge. This enabled him to bring London's refuse for burning and to use the ashes in the production of a cheaper grade of brick. Up to a few years ago, the disused railway, overgrown with weeds, could be seen at Cook's level crossing.

Cook died at Knowle Hill Park on 2 February 1904; he left annuities to all his employees, but most of his estate went to hospitals and charities.

After Cook's death, the brickworks were renamed Oxshott Brickworks Ltd, and brick-making continued under new management, chairman W. E. Benton, and directors N. M. Benton and W. A. Collins.

The brickyard was requisitioned in both world wars to house Canadian soldiers. During the Second War, the office was moved to Perran, Beaconsfield Road, Claygate.

When the Canadians vacated the works at the end of the war, production was resumed but dwindled over the years and finally ceased in 1958. When the pumps stopped, the clay pits filled up with water and became a lake. The lake is said to be about one hundred feet deep, making it suitable for sub-aqua diving. The brickworks were bought by Mr Mills of Lancaster and demolished, but the chimney — a landmark — remained until 1967, when it was dynamited on a misty and rainy morning. The site was developed for the Somerville Road housing estate.

There was also a smaller brickworks of some five acres alongside Knipp Hill which, at that time, was called Donkey Lane. Henry Wilfred Scriven of Tudor Court, Fairmile Park Road, was the proprietor and produced about 1,500 hand-made bricks per man per day. The business continued for approximately 40 years and stopped production in 1939. Up to 1957, it remained an open field, where horses grazed and traces of the old kiln could be seen in the top corner. The site was purchased by a Mr Goldsmidt, who built the Pony Chase housing estate.

Tudor Court had vast grounds covering Heath Ridge Green and Links Green Way. In the 1950s, some of the grounds were sold for houses. One of the first was Four Winds, a bungalow with a large garden. It is the house of the poetess, Barbara Garner. At that time, not everyone had a motor car, and it was customary to have only one garage or car port with quite an extensive garden. Nowadays 'luxury' houses with two or more garages and two or more bathrooms with, as Barbara says, 'pocket handkerchief' size gardens, are the norm.

135

Near Tudor Court, there was the public house, the Griffin, which is now a private house, thanks to Mr Scriven, who was a teetotaller.

Knipp Hill Farm was part of the Tudor Court Estate, and is now South Lodge. In 1294, it was the home of William Ate Kneppe. The word Knipp is derived from *cnaepp*, meaning hillock. The old part of South Lodge is the farm cottage, the front of which was built about 100 years ago from Scriven's bricks.

During World War II, South Lodge was requisitioned to house land army girls and, after the war, it became the home of Sir Patrick Nairne and his family.

Cook's brickies; L to R standing: Brown (Manager), Grey, Cotterel, Neale, Jones, Brown, Cotterel, Steadman and Busby; seated: Farrow (carpenter), Hascomb, Rev Waldegrave, Rev Peake (Chaplain of Cook's Iron Hut), Brown and Wells.

ABOVE: Cook's 80th Birthday, 1903; L to R standing:
Abbot (agent), Kate Ayling, Rev Waldegrave, J. E. Cook,
Brown (Manager), Miss Stoton (Sunday School organist);
seated: Mrs Abbott, ?, Mrs J. E. Cook, ?. BELOW: The
brickwork chimney just before it was demolished.

137

140ft. Chimney Is Toppled

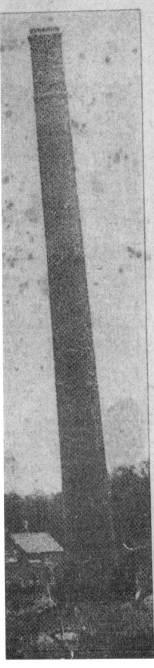

The chimney at Oxshott brickworks—a familiar sight f
so many years—fell majestically to its doom on Wednesd
afternoon.

Gelignite was used to accomplish the task of demolitie
and a two-man team fitted the charges strategically at the b.
of the 140ft. chimney. The detonation was scheduled for 2
p.m. precisely—two or three minutes after a train had pas
safely by the site.

There was a dull boom as the plunger was pressed, and
shout of "There she goes" as the chimney toppled gracefu

Seconds later it was lying as a heap of rubble on
ground. All had gone according to plan.

The many children who had gathered to watch the deme
tion were soon swarming over the pile and more than one sn
boy was seen walking home with a brick as a souvenir of
occasion.

OPPOSITE: Toppling of the chimney. ABOVE: Nos 1 &
2, Brickfield Cottages in Little Heath Lane (demolished
July 1995). BELOW: Replacement 'luxury' houses, 1996.

ABOVE: Jessop's Well. BELOW: Oxshott Woods.

COVERTS AND HEATH

One of the largest woodlands within 20 miles of London and an easy walk to the east of Oxshott, is Prince's Coverts, thickly wooded and of great natural beauty. Prince's Coverts covers over 800 acres and includes Birch Wood, Lime Kiln Wood, Holyroyd's Plantation, Great Oaks, Sixty Acre Wood, New Wood and Stoke Wood. The whole of the Coverts is in the Elmbridge Borough with the exception of Sixty Acre Wood which lies within the Royal Borough of Kingston upon Thames.

Prince's Coverts was originally farm and waste land forming part of Stoke Common. Oaks were planted in the early 1800s, but most of the mature trees were felled during the two world wars. After the Second War, replanting was mainly with conifers, but nowadays, restocking following felling is largely with broad leaf trees.

The Coverts was part of the personal property of Prince Leopold, which the Crown purchased in 1867. It was the Prince's hunting ground when he was resident at Claremont in Esher; hence its name.

Prince's Coverts is noted for its flora and fauna. There is a wide variety of plants, trees and fungi, also wild animals, birds and butterflies. Deer, foxes, rabbits, squirrels and grass snakes are plentiful. A multitude of wrens, robins, sparrows, blackbirds, jays, magpies, woodcocks, woodpeckers, yaffles, thrushes and other birds nest there. Several species of butterflies such as the Purple Emperor, Purple Hairstreak and White Admiral are to be found in the Coverts.

Some parts of the Coverts are of considerable ecological interest. In summer the woods are ablaze with colour and the woodland floor is carpeted with rare species of flowers, including spotted orchids *Dactylorchis Fuchsii* and the purple orchid *Orchis Mascula*. There is an abundance of common bluebells, wood anemone and wild strawberries.

A number of streams and drainage channels criss-cross the woods. There is a small pond near Jessop's Well which is neglected and appears in a sorry state, but some aquatic plants still grow in and around it.

Prince's Coverts is strictly private property and the entrance gates are kept locked. Permits are required for walking and riding. A permit and the key to open the gates are obtainable from the Crown Estate Commissioners for a refundable deposit of £5. There is a public bridle way north of Fairoak Lane, passing alongside Lime Kiln Wood, Birch Wood and Great Oaks, but access to the body of the woodlands is not allowed.

Jessop's Well.   Early maps also show Jessop's Well in Stoke Wood in Prince's Coverts. The well was discovered in the eighteenth century by a Mr Jessop. He built a squat red and brown brick pump room with a pyramidal plain tiled roof. It is a single-storey, Grade II building with a planked door in the south side and an arched window opening with iron bars to the north.

Jessop's Well is hidden among trees and shrubs, adjoining a track called the Avenue, which is not far from what used to be called Steer Lane towards the Oxshott end of Fairoak Lane.

Romans believed in medicinal properties of some waters to cure gout, arthritis and some other ailments, and spas were developed to 'take waters'. Some people drank the water and others bathed in it. Many people, even nowadays, believe in the curative properties of spa waters.

The waters of Jessop's Well are chalybeate (iron-rich) and have strong purgative characteristics. The well was cleaned on 16 October 1729 and produced 160 gallons a day, but the poor worker who stood bare-legged for three hours in the water was purged for seven days. The well was cleaned again in 1848 with equally disastrous results. Over the years, it fell into disrepair until it was restored in 1931.

The medicinal properties of the water were claimed to be superior to those of Cheltenham. Dr Swithin Adee of Guildford wrote in 1749 that he had found advantageous and uncommon effects from the use of the waters of Jessop's Well. It cured people of obstinate scurvies and he was satisfied that 'judicious use of the water would act smartly and that cautious use of it had happy consequences'. Samuel Pepys has recorded in his diaries going to the well for 'taking waters'. Legend has it that bottles of the water were supplied to Henry VIII at 3d each. Bottles were sold at Owens Mineral Water Warehouse at Temple Bar in Fleet Street, London, at 6d each.

Mr Jessop tried to develop a spa around his well but his efforts came to nothing as Epsom beat him to the line. Maintenance of the well is now the responsibility of the Crown Estates Commissioners. Jessop's Well was listed in 1953 as being of special architectural and historical interest.

Oxshott Heath.   One of the beautiful areas of open space accessible to all and sundry, without restriction and without any charge, is Oxshott Heath covering about 190 acres of woodland and heath. Local residents exercise their dogs, go horse riding or just walking. Standing on top of the Heath near the War Memorial, it is hard to believe that London is less than 20 miles away. At times, it looks devoid of habitation, as it was a century and a half ago.

142

The Heath's soil is siliceous sand, unsuitable for farm crops, but coarse grass, gorse, heather and pine thrive there. Yellow sand of the Bagshot Beds is capped by flint gravel and patches of London Clay are visible to the east of the Common towards Sandy Lane.

A path going southwards leads to the edge of the Oxshott plateau and to the stone War Memorial built after the First World War by Sir Malcolm McAlpine of Fairmile Court, Cobham. There are fine views from there of the Mole basin and the Dorking gap.

Oxshott Heath is in the Manor of Esher and Milbourne and was a part of the Claremont Estate. When Queen Victoria bought part of the estate, which included the Manor, she became Lord of the Manor.

A Mrs Louise Vedy wrote on 23 July 1894 requesting permission to take a horse-drawn van on to the Heath to erect a marquee and sell refreshments on the occasion of a children's 'Band of Hope' outing. The Crown Estate Commissioners then managed the Heath, although the soil was vested in the Queen as Lord of the Manor. Mrs Vedy's letter was forwarded to the Queen's solicitor who turned down the request as Napper already had a marquee for the same purpose. Since 1923, the Lordship has been vested in Elmbridge Council.

With the opening in 1885 of the railway station next to the Heath, it became a favourite place for picnickers, day trippers and organised children's groups. It was also frequented by gypsies, fair ground followers and tramps. Prior to 1904, there was no control or supervision of any sort and considerable damage to trees and heather took place. The worried residents of Oxshott petitioned the Ministry of Agriculture and Fisheries to preserve the Heath as a beauty spot. After a Public Inquiry and a lengthy Parliamentary procedure, including a House of Commons Select Committee, which heard evidence from prominent local residents, B. P. Ellis of Bevendean and Sir Ernest Spencer MP of Warren Mount (Robin Hill), the Commons Regulations (Oxshott) Provisional Order Act was promulgated in July 1904. It vested the control and management in a body of nine Conservators; one to be appointed by the Lord/Lady of the Manor, one by the Commissioners of Woods and Forests (Commissioners for Crown Lands), two by Cobham Parish Council (Elmbridge Council), and the remaining five elected, at a public meeting to be held every third year by residents living within one and a half miles of Oxshott railway bridge, who had subscribed not less than ten shillings (50p) to the Heath Fund.

The first Conservators were Sir Robert Collins, John Henry Clutton, Alfred Dawson, Basil Pym Ellis (Chairman), James J. Morrish, Sir Ernest Spencer, George Trollope, Louis Verrey and

143

George G. Vertue (Hon Clerk). The current Conservators are T. B. Altham, H. Crawford (Chairman), R. H. Garlick, I. Gorwyn, E. F. Kirby, B. Parker, D. Prince, D. W. Small and Mrs J. P. Travers.

The Conservators elect a Chairman, Hon Clerk, Hon Treasurer, and Hon Ranger, all of whom play an important role in the management of the Heath. The Hon Clerk has always been a resident who is also a practising solicitor. The present one is G. P. White.

The Heath is one of the few places where truffles may be found. French and Italian restaurateurs from Soho, London, are known to dig out the truffles, using trained dogs.

A man nicknamed Ferney used to visit the Heath almost daily in the autumn to gather brown bracken and take it away in large sacks. Since the Heath at that time was Crown property, the local policeman, PC Ivy, who had not made a single arrest so far, one day arrested him for unlawfully removing Crown property. Ferney was found guilty and fined. The local paper headlined the event 'P C Ivy Clings'.

On the east side of the Heath towards Warren Lane, there is a largish pit from which sand was extracted for building purposes. Sand was also used to fill bags to reinforce buildings that might be bombed in wartime.

During both world wars, Canadians used parts of the Heath for their training, and live ammunition was used near the sandpit.

Every weekend in the summer, visitors come in their hundreds by train, coach and car, bringing their packed lunch and tea. All day they walk through the woods, or play games or just sleep under the trees or sun themselves on the Heath. They depart leaving empty cans, bottles, paper and plastic wrappers and bags, cigarette packets and newspapers. They do not contribute a penny to the cost of clearance or maintenance of the Heath.

People who look after the Heath do a remarkably difficult job with few resources. Throughout the year, trees have to be looked after, ditches cleared and all obstructions on paths and horse-rides removed to keep the Heath tidy and in good condition. This work is carried out mainly by a full-time warden assisted by volunteers.

All this costs a great deal of money and the Conservators rely almost entirely on subscriptions, mainly from residents of Oxshott and neighbouring villages and towns. Although Elmbridge Council owns the Heath, its fixed annual grant is only £150 and a variable donation averaging about £1,000 per annum. Sometimes the Commissioners of Crown Lands and the Forestry Commission make small grants.

The Conservators augment their revenue by selling timber but there is a limit to that. They make some money by allowing film, television and advertising companies to use the Heath in their projects.

Among the films shot in and around the sandpit was *Jew Suss* in 1934, starring Conrad Veidt and *The Forbidden Territory* with Anthony Bushell. Films starring Marty Feldman and Omar Shariff were made at the Heath as also was the TV series *Jabberwocky*.

The hurricane of 16 October 1987 brought untold havoc. A great number of mature trees were uprooted, horse-rides and paths were blocked. The railway line from Cook's Crossing was also blocked. Clearing of the railway line and main roads was done swiftly, but rather slowly along many verges and in the woods. Many areas in the Heath were untouched a year later. Hardly had the mess been cleared away when more gales arrived in January 1990. That put further strain on the already slim resources but, with prudent management and patience, the Heath has recovered.

The Refreshment Hut. Napper's marquee catered for children and visitors to the Heath. When the First World War broke out, all visits ceased and so did Napper's activities. After the war, Napper sold his business to Manser, who did not revive it. Miss Gertrude Mill, her sister and her friend, Gurner Rimmer, filled the gap. Gertrude brought a large wooden army hut from Southport and erected it on railway land facing the station adjoining the Heath. The Conservators were none too happy as they feared that people would take food and drinks onto the Heath and leave behind litter and broken glass. The Railway Company accepted the Conservators' proposal to impose a condition that all refreshments would be consumed on the premises, and food in paper bags and bottled liquids to be taken away, would not be sold.

The simple café — not so simple from its interior arrangement — was highly popular with visitors and crowded at the weekends, although it was open throughout the year. Canadian soldiers appreciated the facilities and she ran the café successfully for about 40 years.

Gurner Rimmer was not involved in the café business. He was an artist of considerable ability and used a nearby small hut as his studio and often slept there. He was well-known locally for his paintings and especially his cartoons. He died tragically one night in his studio hut when it was gutted by fire through an overturned oil stove. The café was also damaged but Gertrude, although heartbroken, carried on for a further four years. However, her heart was no longer in the business and she sold it to W. Parkin from Epsom who had an ice cream business at the racecourse. After a few years, he died in Spain, convalescing. His widow carried on the business until the middle of 1980 when the building was totally destroyed by a fire. Then there was only a small hut serving light refreshments, but that too is now gone.

Gipsies' Corner, Oxshott.

ABOVE: View of Oxshott from the top of the heath.
BELOW: Canadian soldiers training in Oxshott Woods
(Lt Ward and carrying party).

147

ABOVE: Gale damage in Oxshott, 1990. BELOW:
Interior of the Refreshment Hut.

COMMUNITY SPIRIT

In spite of being a small village, Oxshott has a wide range of cultural and sports activities other similar villages might well envy.

The Mothers' Union

Although church-related, the Mothers' Union was founded in 1896 but it did not arrive in Oxshott until sixteen years later. The Vicar, Rev Skene, chaired a meeting in October 1912 to inaugurate the Oxshott Branch. It was attended by 37 'working class' and 10 'lady members' and Mrs Skene of the Parsonage was appointed secretary. The first mention of the branch is in the Official Handbook of the Union in 1913. However, mothers must have been meeting some years before, since Smith Charity's records reveal small grants to their meetings in Oxshott from 1900 to 1903 and again in 1911. The objects at that time were to 'uphold the sanctity of marriage; to awaken in mothers of all classes a sense of their great responsibility as mothers in the training of their boys and girls (the future fathers and mothers of the Empire); and to organise in every place a band of mothers who will unite in prayer and seek by their own example to lead their family in purity and holiness of life'.

Originally the Mothers' Union was only open to married women with children but in 1912 its constitution was amended to admit unmarried women as associate members. Childless married women had the option to become full or associate members as they wished. That option, however, was withdrawn in 1926.

The membership is not restricted to members of the Church of England. Recently the constitution has been amended. Divorcees and single persons with or without children are admitted and men are welcomed. The Bishop of Guildford, Rt Rev John Gladwin, says 'The Mothers' Union must belong to the modern world, meeting the needs of the modern world today'.

Dioceses at that time did not pay a subscription to headquarters based on membership, as is done now, but sent a voluntary donation. It is not clear whether members paid a subscription to their branch or to the diocese. The current honorary secretary of the Oxshott branch is Mrs Sonia Sharman.

The Women's Institute

The inaugural meeting of the Oxshott branch of The Women's Institute was on 17 July 1919 with 65 women attending. Its aims were practical, educational, cultural and social. Oxshott in those days was a tiny village with big houses in vast grounds and each with a large number of servants. Being a servant or poor was no bar to membership.

Mrs Alice Northcott was elected President with Mrs Skeeton Vice President. Mrs Sybil Morrish and Mrs Reed were appointed Hon Secretary and Treasurer respectively.

The Institute became so popular that within four months the membership had reached 130, the maximum permitted being 140. Among the founding members were Florence Brown and her friend Evelyn Lowe. Seventy years later, Florence, by then Mrs Ratcliffe, was still attending meetings regularly; Evelyn became the well-known 'Norah' Brown of Brown's Corner and, like her friend, continued to participate.

Meetings were held in the old Church Hall to which a club room was later added. At first, talks and classes were on domestic subjects such as cookery, dressmaking and needlework. Lively meetings were followed by recorded music, singing, dancing and musical chairs. In the Institute's Minutes of the November 1919 meeting is recorded the sudden arrival of the Vicar to warn of an approaching storm. The ladies fled 'without the usual dancing'. Most would have come on foot as few had cars or could drive.

Miss Vernon, the Surrey County Oganiser, rebuked the Oxshott branch in January 1920 saying that it 'was inclined to be only for amusement'. Since then the range of activities has widened, its members have won prizes for singing, choral and public speaking, drama, essay writing, needlework, embroidery, cookery and painting. Paintings by Mrs Elizabeth Lee have been 'hung' at the Royal Academy exhibitions and those of Miss Alice Grey were a regular feature for several years at the Arts and Crafts Exhibition. Its collage 'Village' of 54 leaves, each depicting an aspect of the village life, hangs in the Village Centre.

The Oxshott Women's Institute has organised visits to theatres, concerts and elsewhere, helps with Christmas Fairs and other events and has raised funds for worthy causes. During World War II, members had allotments in the grounds of Danes Court Domestic Science School. They made several thousand pounds of jam in a garage in Oakshade Road and bought and operated a canning machine. They also ran a daily canteen for Canadian soldiers and gave them hospitality in their homes.

The branch, now called the Oxshott Afternoon Women's Institute, is a founder member of the Yvonne Arnaud Theatre at Guildford. It has been so successful that two others, the Oxshott Evening and Oxshott Village, have been established. Mrs Pat Forsyth was appointed secretary in the 1950s and continued until she left the village in 1990. Mrs E. M. Hughes took over.

Women's Institute in Oxshott have achieved the Objectives set in 1919. The Institute's banner, copied by a group of members in 1994, replaced the original one. It bears on a blue background the inspiring caption 'Work, Joy, Wisdom'. To quote one of the members, 'Work we accomplish, Joy we experience, to Wisdom we can only aspire'.

Scouts and Guides

Scouting came to Oxshott in 1912, five years after Lord Robert Baden-Powell had established the movement nation-wide. At the suggestion of Miss Ida Verrey of The Warren in Warren Lane, George Stoton, the headmaster of the Royal Kent School, formed the first group. Miss Ida Verrey and her two sisters, Dora and Hettie, helped with training. F. R. Stedman, a leader of Kingston Scouts, was the first Scouter, soon to be joined by George Brown and Stanley Taylor. At first, the green iron hut in the school grounds was used as the scout hut. The boys met for training and kept their kit in the hut. Later The Warren was used for meetings with training in its grounds and the kit stored in the garages. Their annual fête was held in the Verreys' large garden. This continued until the death of Ida, the last surviving member of the family.

Oxshott Scouts have managed to survive even when their number was reduced to one for lack of Scouters during the last war. However, in 1943 Miss Mary Frank restarted Wolf Cubs (now called Cub Scouts), with twelve small boys. The Pack grew quickly and soon afterwards a troop of boy scouts was also formed. Miss Franch continued as Cub Master until 1961. Cliff Skinner, one of her Cubs, led Oxshott Scouts for several years until he left the area in 1967. There were 37 Scouts, eight Rovers and 35 Cubs in 1965. Continuous growth led to a second pack. Mrs P. Trinder was the Cub leader in the eighties and the two packs are now led by Peter Lemmon. There is also a Beaver Scouts pack catering for boys aged six to eight years led by Ms Paula Scrivens. Many of them, on reaching the age limit, join the Cubs and most of them, on reaching 10½ years of age become Scouts. Scouts have been led by Richard Coveney for several years. Oxshott also has a Venture Scouts group for 15 to 20 year olds and its leader is John Christmas.

Robin Salter, one time senior Scout Leader of 1st Oxshott, and Scout Leader in HM Forces in Germany and at the School of Infantry, Warminster, was appointed in 1970 District Commissioner for Esher, which embraced the Oxshott scouts. He had been Assistant District Commissioner for six years and awarded a long-service decoration and the medal of merit. The three Misses Verrey remained the patrons of Oxshott Scouts till their deaths.

151

The most important event in the history of Oxshott Scouts was the establishment of a permanent camp in 1920 at Polyapes, Stoke D'Abernon, on a site donated by the Phillips family. Oxshott Scouts since then have held their annual camps there. Scouts from other areas too have often used the site for their camps and fêtes.

A memorial dedicated to boy scouts, built on the site by Sir Robert McAlpine of Fairmile Court, Cobham, is a bronze statue of a scout by A. P. Burton, cast at the Bronze Foundry in Thames Ditton.

The word *Polyapes*, according to W. T. Bishop, is derived from two words — 'Poly' is an abbreviation of 'Pollard' and 'Apes' stands for 'Aspen'. Aspen trees abounded in the area and were usually 'Polled' meaning stowed. However, in 1846 Polyapes was called Holy Harps, and the name of the meadow below it was Roundabouts.

Another milestone of the movement was the building of a new headquarters at the southern end of Waverley Road in 1968. Scouts collected nearly £1,600 and Guides £1,350 and the Council gave a grant of £1,500 towards the cost. The opening ceremony was performed by Miss Ida, the longest surviving Verrey sister. The headquarters are appropriately named the Verrey Hut. Miss Ida died in 1974.

Brownies

Oxshott had its first Brownie Pack in 1922. Mrs Hoskyns of Woodside Road was Brown Owl in 1924 and two cousins, Margaret and Joyce Gray, were in the Pack. Margaret is Mrs Margaret Willcox of Crown Cottages, Steels Lane and Joyce is Joyce Elliott of Blundel Lane. The pack was disbanded in 1935.

A new pack was formed and registered in June 1940 with Miss Fletcher Rose as Brown Owl. Mrs Dora McIntosh was a recent leader who led the Brownies for 15 years until her death in 1964. Mrs Sonia Sharman has been its leader for several years. The Pack celebrated its Golden Jubilee in 1990. A second Pack was formed in 1964, its leader, Miss Wendy Simmonds; the current leader is Mrs Rose Williams.

Guides

The 1st Oxshott Guides Company started in 1920. Its captain was Miss Suckling-Baron and it was disbanded in 1927.

After a lapse of six years, Miss M. Thompson established a new 1st Oxshott Guides Company. Miss Thompson was captain of the 2nd Cobham (Sandroyd) Guides, which had disbanded in 1933 after seven years' existence. Those Oxshott girls who were in the disbanded company were happy to become the backbone of the new 1st Oxshott Company. (Sandroyd is now called Reed's School). The Company was registered on 22 February 1933.

Initially there were four patrols, each consisting of six guides. They met and drilled in the Sports Club's grounds, went tracking and stalking on the Heath and cooked meals in gardens of various large houses. Since their number was small, they joined companies from other areas to go camping and participate in rallies at Albury Park, often comprising some 3,000 Guides. At one of these, the Oxshott Company won a 1st Certificate.

The Company was reduced to 12 guides during the last war and their activities perforce curtailed. They met on Saturday afternoons and dispersed half an hour before the blackout in the winter. They helped the war effort by collecting loads of 'silver' foil, delivering it on a trek cart to the station, sending parcels to the submarine HMS *Shark* and to the Blind School. At the end of the War, the 1st Oxshott Guides Company consisted of three Guiders, 18 Guides and six holiday members who came home from boarding schools. The Company grew to 40 Guides and has had its maximum permitted number for several years.

The Guides helped to clear the site and decorate the interior of their new headquarters in Waverley Road which were built in 1968.

Joyce Gray, one of the first Brownies in the village, duly graduated to become a Guide. Her father, William Gray, was the head gardener at Willoughbys mansion in Leatherhead Road. During the last war she married Mr Elliott, one of the Canadian army men stationed in Oxshott. However, she continued to work for the welfare and advancement of Oxshott Guides and became their captain. Later her merits and work were recognised by the London Headquarters and she was appointed Assistant District Commissioner. She was awarded the MBE in 1976 for her services to Guides. Although now retired, living in Blundel Lane, Stoke D'Abernon, she is still actively interested in the Guides Movement. The current Guide Leader is Mrs E. Twist.

Another Oxshottian connected with the Guides is the ex-treasurer of FEDORA, Edward Holding of Birdshill Farmhouse in Warren Lane. He is the hon treasurer of the Guides Associaton of the United Kingdom.

The Oxshott Club

Until almost the end of the eighteenth century, residents in Oxshott were too few and too poor to think of recreation. They worked long hours and did not have time or facilities. Sundays were no exception as they had chores to perform. Even in 1877, there were only 29 houses in the whole of Oxshott.

The picture started to change with the arrival of the railway in 1885, and soon thereafter the building of stately mansions. Wealthy owners had a large number of servants, and considered it prudent to provide recreation facilities. They encouraged their staff to meet and socialise. Initially Rev Copson Peake's iron hut in the grounds of the Royal Kent School was used for meetings and some indoor games but that was not satisfactory. It was decided in 1907 to establish a Working Men's Club in a suitable building which could be used also as a parish hall, since the temporary church built in 1904 had none. R. J. Lambert of Danes Hill donated the present site, together with a substantial sum towards the cost of a building. The land was formally conveyed to Rev A. S. P. Blackburne, rector of St Mary's at Stoke D'Abernon on 4 October 1907. R. Ashford Dash of Englefield, B. P. Ellis of Bevendean, W. E. Faulkner of Midgarth and L. C. Verrey of the Warren were among founder-members. All of them, except Mr Ellis, served as president of the Club for several years. Mr Ellis's widow, son Whitaker and son-in-law, Trevor Castle, made donations. Rev F. N. Skene and G. G. Vertue of Birds Hill Drive worked hard to raise funds. Local builders, H. G. & A. Osman Ltd built the clubhouse at a cost of £454 12s 2d (£454.61). The first president was the Rector, Rev A. S. P. Blackburne.

A billiards table was installed and facilities for other indoor games such as darts and cards, together with a small library and a bar. The present billiards room also became the Parish Room and was the venue for Mrs Bowen Buscarlet's tea party on 25 October 1911 to celebrate the laying of the Foundation Stone of St Andrew's Church. It was attended by HRH the Duchess of Albany, the Lord Lieutenant of the County, the Bishop of Winchester, Rev Skene and other dignitaries.

The Club was soon well established and billiards was the most popular game.

One of the Club's best players was 'Arty' Simmons who, in 1913 when still a teenager, won the Club's championship and retained the title for the following three years. He won again five times between 1919 and 1927, and again five times successively from 1928 to 1933. The Club then awarded him 'The Cup for Keeps'. Mr Simmons was also a good footballer.

Another excellent billiards player was Arnold Trinder who continued to support the Club up to his death in 1940.

The Club went through difficulties in both World Wars. After the last war, John Palmer of Unicorn Cottage and of Rendel Palmer & Tritton, consulting engineers, was president and a considerable supporter. The current president is Richard Hockin.

After the 1939-45 war, the word 'Working' was dropped from the name, which became Oxshott Men's Club and more recently, in the fashion of today, it is simply the Oxshott Club.

Oxshott Village Sports Club

Although it is generally believed that Oxshott Village Sports Club was founded in 1919, its origin goes back to the nineteenth century when cricket was played on a field belonging to Canon Phillips' family in Stoke D'Abernon which included Oxshott. Probably the Club was formed in 1870 when matches were played against Bookham and the Tilt. There is also a record of a match against West Clandon in 1892. George Stoton, headmaster of the Royal Kent School, was an active member. The local Council acquired the field and adjacent land in the 1930s, which is now known as Stoke D'Abernon Recreation Ground.

When Bevendean was built for Basil Pym Ellis in 1898, its ground provided cricket and football pitches with pavilions. The cricket ground was at the other end of Sheath Lane, at the corner of what is now Goldrings Road. The arrival of R. J. Lambert at Danes Hill in 1901 gave a boost to the sport.

Matches at the weekend were a regular feature of village life. Many leading county, 'varsity' and public school cricketers took part. Special occasions were the matches on Whit Monday and August Bank Holiday. The Lamberts mustered a team against Oxshott on Whit Monday at Danes Hill whereas Bevendean was the venue for the Ellis' match on August Bank Holiday. Peculiarly, Basil Ellis who, with his beard resembled the famous cricketer W. G. Grace, always played at this match for Oxshott against his own team. Marquees were put up on these occasions and the hosts provided tea, lunch and supper. An impromptu concert rounded off the day.

Players included Mr Ellis' son Whitaker, his son-in-law Trevor Castle, his head gardener W. Bailey, another gardener, Edwards of Fairmile and his son and the Wadey brothers Mark, Luke and Jesse. Trevor Castle was the wicketkeeper and Whitaker was a formidable batsman.

A regular fixture was the match between the Whips and the Spades. The Whips were coachmen and the Spades, gardeners of the village wealthy.

All the players were amateurs and there were no subscriptions or fees to pay. The maintenance and upkeep costs of grounds and equipment were met by rich owners.

Outdoor sport more or less came to a halt on the death of Basil Ellis in 1907. Bevendean was put up for sale by auction in 1908 and the grounds were no longer available. Cricket at Danes Hill met the same fate by the death of Mr Lambert in 1915. Most young men were called up and activities were suspended until the end of the war.

They were revived in 1919-20 largely through the efforts of Arnold Trinder, J. P. Tilley, H. F. Taylor and other owners of large properties. The Steels Lane site was leased from the Crown with Mr Trinder underwriting the annual ground rent of nearly £100.

Grounds were laid out for one asphalt and three grass tennis courts, a cricket pitch and a three rink bowling green. Wooden buildings were erected in different parts of the grounds along the eastern boundary for each sport and the old Bevendean pavilion was re-assembled to become the bowls hut. The first turf for the cricket pitch was laid by Mr Tilley ably assisted by Harry Gray and N. C. Champness. Mr Gray was a groom at St Mary's Cottage where one of the hunts used to meet.

The Steels Lane entrance was a muddy potholed lane until the late 1960s when it was concreted. There was a much used narrow footpath from Oakshade Road immediately adjoining the northern wall of Oxshott Men's Club to the Village Sports Club.

During 1924 and 1925 cricket at Oxshott was of such a high quality that the former England and Surrey captain H. D. G. Leverson Gower brought teams of 'test cricket' standard to play against Oxshott. Jack Hobbs, Andy Sandham of Surrey, J. H. Douglas of England and Essex and M. W. Tate and E. H. Bowley of England and Sussex were among those who played here.

Arnold Trinder lent a substantial sum to the Club in the mid-1930s to purchase the freehold, which has a restrictive covenants, if ever the grounds cease to be used as a sports club, the Crown has first refusal to repurchase.

During the 1939-45 war, activities were restricted although all three sections remained operative. In 1943, it organised a horticultural show and fête which raised £900 for the British Red Cross Society. It became an annual event but, from the end of the war in 1945 to the twentieth fête in 1962, half of the net income was donated to the Oxshott Trust Fund and the other half retained by the Club to restore, improve and expand playing facilities.

Since the wooden huts were unsuitable for indoor social activities, an ex-Canadian army hut from Oxshott Brick Works was purchased and refurbished to provide a licensed bar. Then it was decided to build a proper pavilion and club house. Generous grants from the Council and the Department of Education and Science enabled the Club to build a new pavilion. It was opened on 12 April 1959 by Sir Charles Trinder, the then Lord Mayor of the City of London, and the son of Arnold Trinder.

The Club since then has expanded considerably and become self-supporting. It is the only multi-sport organisation within easy reach of residents of Oxshott, Cobham, Claygate and Esher. There are now nine tennis courts, a full-sized six rink bowling green, and first class cricket fields for two XIs and a colt team of juniors. The Club also has two squash courts and sections for archery, hockey, netball, football and bridge. It encourages younger members and has a professional tennis coach. The bridge section accepts novices.

A general committee is responsible for the overall management with sectional committees for each sport. Arnold Trinder was president for 20 years from 1920 until his death in 1940, followed by J. P. Tilley for 10 years to 1951. R. C. (Jack) Tarring was hon secretary for 18 years and then president from 1971 to 1974.

The Birdshill Group

Oxshottians usually sought relaxation and culture in London but, with restricted travel facilities, air raids and black-outs during the Second World War, Hilton Thorpe, a prominent resident, suggested a substitute. He proposed that they meet in the evenings to talk and socialise. The idea caught on and the Birdshill Group came into being. The first meeting was on 3 October 1944 at The Ridge in Birdshill Drive, Mr and Mrs Hilton Thorpe's home (later at Southlands, Fairoak Lane). It was an informal gathering talking about 'What should be done with the Germans'.

Presumably the Group acquired its name from Mr Thorpe's address. Typically British, and like Britain, it had no written constitution. It was as informal as it could be. It had no rules or regulations and its chairman and secretary were not elected but took on the duties voluntarily. Membership was by invitation only. Mr Thorpe carried out the chairman's work and, after a time, Miss H. M. Crown took on the administrative work as hon secretary. Upon Mr Hilton's death, Jack Woollcombe of Hemerton, Danes Way (later Fairoaks, Fairoak Lane), assumed chairmanship and continued until he moved away from Oxshott. Then Irving Todd, of Broad Highway, Cobham, took over.

Soon after its formation, the Government asked local councils to encourage local fire-guard units to form 'moots', reporting their discussions to authorities to enable the government to keep in touch with public opinion on local and national matters.

Oxshott had four moots but their activities did not impinge on the Birdshill Group as they were concerned with local matters, whereas the Group was interested in social and cultural subjects only.

The Group met in the houses of those members who could accommodate 20 to 25 persons. At first, the meetings were on full moon days as air raids were not expected, but were switched to dark nights when Jerry became more adventurous and aggressive. The gatherings became a monthly event.

Speakers were usually well-known people living in or near Oxshott and talks were on a wide range of subjects. For example, Sir Adrian Boult talked on Music and Conducting; astronomer, E. H. Noon, gave several talks on his speciality; E. R. Thompson OBE, parliamentary correspondent of the BBC, spoke on Town Planning, also on the House of Lords; Dr T. W. Chalmers on The Lost Atlantis; P. J. Copeland on Tea; F. V. Brilles on Margarine; Barrister J. F. Burns at separate meetings on Duties of a Barrister, Law, the British Army of the Rhine and Education; D. C. Dring on Lord Byron; leader writer J. R. McMillan on The Press and the People; Miss Rosemary Wren on Clay in relation to Pottery Forms; Charles Hogg on Drinking Water with Difficulty; Gordon Budd on The Egypt of Farouk and After.

All the speakers were local. Some of the other important people who addressed the Group were R. L. Atkinson on The Doomsday Book and Onwards; Dr. E. Higgins of the British Museum on the Elgin Marbles, and at another meeting on Greek and Roman Jewellery; Royal Navy Captain, G. Allen on Personal Reminiscences of Winston Churchill; Past Chairman of the Monopolies and Restrictive Practices Commission, Sir David Cairns on Monopolies; Wing Commander Kellet on the Battle of Britain; Group Captain D. J. Sherlock on National Service; G. Frank on Some Aspects of Resistance; Major Rickman (Robin Goodfellow of the *Daily Mail*) on Horse Racing; J. S. Tritton, past President of the Institute of Locomotive Engineers, on Our Railways — Can we afford them. *The railway talk was on 29 March 1962 and the debate is not over yet.*

There were interesting and amusing talks with slides and/or films by F. V. Brilles, C. Hogg, R. C. Tarring, P. Summersgill on their travels. One of the most fascinating films was by Charles Hogg on the Erupting Volcanoes of Hawaii.

At the end of the talks, members were entertained to food and drinks and then came discussion.

December meetings were usually a sort of Christmas party but for unknown reasons were discontinued after that of 12 December 1952. The Birdshill Group appears to have faded away in the mid 1970s.

Oxshott Men's Group

Oxshott Men's Group was founded in 1981 at the suggestion of St Andrew's Vicar, Rev John Green, to enable retired professional men to make new contacts and friends. It operates more or less on similar lines to the Birdshill Group. The membership is open to men only who are retired and, as it meets in St Andrew's Church Hall, the number is limited by the seating capacity of the hall. The membership at present totals 90 with a waiting list. The Vicar is an *ex-officio* member.

A Chairman is appointed for three years and an Hon Secretary/Treasurer whose term of office is indefinite. David N. Dring of Meadway and Gerald Scott, Oakshade Road, are the current Chairman and Secretary/Treasurer. The Group meets every third Wednesday of the month at about 10.30 am with a guest speaker at 11 am. At the end of the meeting, the Group has a ploughman's lunch. There is an outing in June and no meeting in August.

O'Brien Club

This Club in Webster Close for old people was formed in November 1948 and is named in memory of Captain J. T. and Mrs O'Brien.

Capt O'Brien first saw Oxshott during the 1914-18 war. After his marriage at the end of the war, he came to reside at Rowhurst Wood, a house built in 1896 with bells in all rooms and bell board in the servants' quarters.

He served on the Stoke D'Abernon Parish Council since 1922 and was its Chairman until its absorption by Esher Urban District Council. He was elected a Councillor in 1933 and was Chairman 1935-37. He was appointed a Justice of Peace in 1923 and MBE for services at the Ministry of Works and to the village.

Mrs O'Brien was active in the Oxshott District Nursing Association and became its Chairman. Later she moved from Rowhurst Wood to Woodside Cottage in Littleheath Lane. She was a manager of the Royal Kent School in 1937.

There is a bench in Blundel Lane in memory of Capt O'Brien.

Oxshott Art & Crafts Society

Although the village had several amateur and professional painters, potters and other craftsmen, there was no organisation to bring them together and popularise their work. Martin Hutchinson and Irving Todd got together and mounted an exhibition of their and some other artists' work at the old St Andrew's Church Hall in 1936. More were intended, but the war intervened and the idea was not revived until 1946. A two-day exhibition was held in 1947 and repeated in 1948 and 1950. The exhibitions were organised by an Art and Crafts Committee headed by Dr T. W. Chalmers and under the auspices of the Oxshott Trust Fund. Local scouts safeguarded the exhibits at night by camping in the Church Hall.

At a crowded meeting held on 25 October 1954 at Potters Croft in Oakshade Road, Oxshott Art & Crafts Society was formally established with the objects to encourage the practice of fine arts and craftsmanship in the village and neighbouring areas and to organise lectures, meetings and exhibitions of work. The membership was open to all who practiced or had an interest in the arts and crafts and the management committee was to represent various arts. The annual subscription for adults was fixed at 7s 6d (37½p) and 2s 6d (12½p) for youngsters under 16. The meeting also decided that members of the management committee must always represent a different art or craft.

A committee was elected with Chairman Irving Todd; Hon Treasurer: Mrs Elsie Hogg; Hon Secretary: Miss Rosemary Wren; Painting: Martin Hutchinson; Pottery: Miss E. H. Pincombe; Wood and Metal: Charles Hogg; Needlework and Weaving: Mrs Rathbone; Ciné and Still Photography: Mrs B. Davis; Dr T. W. Chalmers was appointed an honorary member in recognition of his work for past exhibitions.

Monthly meetings of the committee were at the Oak Tea Room.

Initially the Society's exhibitons were held as part of the annual fête organised by the Oxshott Trust Fund on the first Saturday in September at the Sports Club's grounds. The exhibition was in a long tent.

The fête was discontinued after a series of wet weather days as the heavy cost of restoring the sports grounds resulted in a loss.

The Art & Crafts Exhibition was resumed in 1962 at the new Village Centre and since then has been held there annually and now biannually. The number of exhibits has increased year after year and a large proportion is sold.

Well-known artists have exhibited, for example (Sir) Patrick Nairne of South Lodge, Knipp Hill, who was Secretary to the First Lord of the Admiralty and later Permanent Secretary at the Ministry of Health. His water colours have been 'hung' at Royal Academy Exhibitions in London; so have the paintings of Mrs Stuart-Lee.

John Foulger was a Royal Air Force pilot shot down in 1942 and confined in Stalag III. He started painting there without having had any previous lessons, using materials supplied by the Red Cross and old kit bags as canvases. Douglas Bader was at the same camp. His paintings have been exhibited in New York and London. John Foulger lived at Southcroft in Spicers Field from 1966 to 1974.

The Society's monthly meetings are held now at the Village Centre when talks and demonstrations are given by professionals, as well as talented and accomplished amateurs, on a wide range of subjects such as the preservation of textiles, the restoration of paintings, theatre design, glass engraving, restoration of old landscape gardens, etc. The Society organises painting classes and outings to places of interest. Its membership exceeds 200.

Potteries

Oxshott had two potteries producing high quality original articles and objects of artistic craft. Neither catered for retail sales, preferring to take their work to galleries and shops in London and other cities and large towns. Although costly compared to mass-produced pottery, appreciative local people came to them for special presents and their occasional workshop exhibitions.

One of the potteries, called Old Forge Pottery, owned by Helen Pincombe, was behind No 1 Dorothy Cottages in Steels Lane. It was previously the smithy, Shoesmith & Lee, where a Mr Russell, blacksmith and farmer, worked before moving to Cobham. Miss Pincombe gave lessons in pottery at the Guildford School of Art, and later at the Royal College of Arts, London. Her work as potter and teacher was widely respected.

The Oxshott pottery at Potters Croft in Oakshade Road was the other one. It was established by Denise and Henry Wren.

Potters Croft was built in 1920 by Denise and Henry Wren with their own hands, with assistance from her two brothers and a friendly builder's firm. It is an eccentric bungalow designed by Denise and planned to be practical, easy to run and maintain and above all inexpensive. She used modern materials. It had a coloured concrete floor with Celtic knot designs which she inlaid herself. The workshop was an ex-army hut in their garden with an American Drakenfield gas-fired muffle kiln. There was no electricity in either the workshop or the bungalow which was lit by gas lights only until 1949. Denise shared the cost of the Drakenfield kiln with two other potters — Miss Gillespie of Cobham and Mrs Laird of Ewell — for an agreed number of firings. Oakshade Road was dug up to install extra large gas pipes for the kiln. Later a traditional flower-pot kiln was built by Mr Mercer of Norbiton Potteries followed by a whole series of others fired with coke and later by gas to Denise's design, but the old Drakenfield remained a reliable standby until the 1950s. Potters Croft was the 127th house in Oxshott.

Denise studied at the Science Arts School at Kingston upon Thames under Manxman Archibald Knox. In 1912 Denise set up her own workshop in one of the rooms of The Knox Guild of Design & Craft at 24A Market Place, Kingston, becoming the first independent woman potter in Britain.

Henry Wren was a journalist by profession, studied watercolour painting under Knox at Wimbledon Arts School and was a freelance reporter for *The Times* and later, personal private secretary to Sir Rupert D'Oyly Carte. Denise and Henry first met in 1913 at an exhibition and married in April 1915.

Denise developed a new technique for fixing richly coloured glazes at 100°C below the usual 1280°C, enabling her to use colours unstable at the higher temperature.

During the First World War, Henry, after serving in the Intelligence Department of the War Office, went to Belgium with the Bedfordshire Regiment. He was wounded at La Panne and returned.

Denise and Harry designed and printed greetings cards under the name of Wren & Wren in London after the war. Then Henry saw an advertisement for plots of land in Oxshott available for sale to returning war veterans. They purchased the land and started the pottery.

Oxshott Pottery organised a stand, shared with other craftsmen, at the British Empire Exhibition at Wembley in 1924 and 1925.

With the threat of war looming in 1938, pottery sales slumped and Denise turned to textile design, selling at Mancheter and to Liberty in London. After the war she returned to pottery, employing Douglas Zadek as a thrower until he started his own pottery in Cobham. In 1958 she designed a coke-fired kiln especially for salt-glaze; it is on this work that her reputation rests. Unfortunately it came to an end when, due to changes in gas technology, the gas works at Leatherhead closed down in 1968 and the correct soft coke fuel became unobtainable. His work is exhibited at the Victoria and Albert Museum.

During the 1939-45 war Henry became a full-time air raid warden and also started the Oxshott Food Growers Association which ploughed up part of the sports ground near the wood to grow potatoes communally. He died in 1947 at the age of 63 while still working at the Institute of Education.

When Henry died, their daughter Rosemary, born in 1922, was still studying at the Guildford School of Art before going on to the Royal College of Arts in London. She took over his workshop. One of her students was David Canter who later became organising secretary of the Craftsmen Potters Association — still the established professional society. Her ceramics of village scenes of Oxshott show how the village looked in the 1950s. Her first exhibition was in 1954 at Heal's in Tottenham Court Road, London. In 1995, she is still exhibiting.

Rosemary was upset by Oxshott's rapid development in the sixties and seventies. She deprecated the loss of so many trees and fields and missed the community spirit of the past. She left Oxshott in 1978 and established the Oxshott Pottery in Devon with her partner

162

Peter Crotty, first at Easterbrook, north of Dartmoor and then at Lustleigh. She moved again in 1990 and the pottery is now just outside Strathpeffer in the Highlands of Scotland. Denise went with them to Devon where she died in 1979 aged 88.

Oxshott & Cobham Music Society

Oxshott has had a music society since shortly before the last war. Meetings were held in the homes of different members and artists were invited to give recitals. The Society expanded and was fortunate in its association with well-known musicians living locally, including Sir Adrian Boult, Ruth Dyson and Jean Stewart. There was a fairly close connection with those concerned with the Leith Hill Festival.

'Bertie' Rimmer and his family came to live in Oxshott at Pinewood House early in 1952. He and his wife were musicians. Before Oxshott, they had lived in Bristol and Lincoln and she was the leader of both the local orchestra in Bristol and the Lincoln Symphony Orchestra.

Soon after their arrival they both joined the committee. Bertie subsequently became chairman. His elder son, George, was also elected to the committee. Mrs Rimmer died in 1955.

At that time, there were six major monthly recitals usually held at the Roman Catholic Church Hall in Steels Lane between September and May. After 1956, these moved to Pinewoods House with its ideal, long, galleried hall.

Well-known artists giving recitals included Moura Lympany, Julian Bream, Harold Lester, Wynford Evans, John Carol Case, Liza Fuchsova, Oda Slobodskaya, Roger Norrington and Joseph Weingarten. Ensembles performing at Pinewood Houe included the Medici String Quartet, the Aeolian Wind Quartet and The Dumka Trio.

Following Bertie Rimmer's death in February 1986, the Music Society has moved to other venues. Concerts and recitals have been held in Esher at Claremont Fan Court School and the Joyce Grenfell Centre, and in Cobham at Reed's School and the Convent of Notre Dame. The Surrey Philharmonic Orchestra with pianist, Amanda Hurton, gave a concert in 1988. Andrew West, who came second in the 1990 Geneva International Piano Competition, was the soloist at the Music Society's concert in October 1994 in St George's Hall, Esher.

Oxshott Scottish Society

Residents of Scottish origin got together in 1958 to form the Oxshott Scottish Society. Membership was open to Scots and anyone

163

with Scottish connections or an interest in Scotland and its culture. James McMillan was chairman and Mrs Margaret Shand hon secretary. They met once a month, usually at the St Andrew's Church Hall in Oakshade Road.

The Society, over the years, arranged talks by such as Graham Hartley of the Scottish Whisky Association on The Spirit of Scotland, C. S. Richenburg of the Patent Office on Protecting your Ideas and Profiting from Innovation, Master Kilt Maker L. Penrose on Tartan and the Kilt, and Lt Col John Kimmins on History of the Corps of Queen's Messengers.

The main event of the year was the Burns Supper. Real haggis was piped in, usually by Pipe Major Charles Galloway.

Regrettably, like many other small local societies, the Oxshott Scottish Society had to disband in 1994 for lack of support from the younger generation. Mrs Margaret Shand, who had continued in the office of hon secretary from the start, died soon after the winding up.

The Astronomical Group

E. H. Noon, Fellow of the Royal Astronomical Society formed this Group. He was the Group's hon secretary in 1965. He lectured at Reed's School and gave several talks to the Birdshill Group. He had erected a telescope in the gardens of Norman Cottage, Pond Piece, which he bequeathed to Reed's School.

Oxshott Preservation Committee

This Committee was formed in 1950 to protect environmental amenities and the Green Belt. Its main function was to influence and persuade Esher Urban District (Elmbridge) Council not to permit ribbon development of small houses in parts of Aylings Farm (the Waverley Road area), and elsewhere in Oxshott. The Committee vetted all planning applications and made representations where appropriate. In January 1954, a new Committee was appointed consisting of N. C. Champness (Chairman), D. C. Dring (Vice-chairman), Mr Croome (Hon Secretary), C. Staples (Hon Treasurer), Capt J. T. O'Brien and Peter Hollins. It operated from Lantern Cottage, the home of the Chairman in Fairoak Lane.

During the sixties, H. Leadbeater of Milk Wood, Stokesheath Road, was in charge. There is no mention of it after 1967.

Federation of Oxshott Residents and Associations (FEDORA)

Oxshott has a number of residents' associations, each endeavouring to protect their members' interests concerning common problems. While the problems varied, all the associations had one thing in common, namely to safeguard the environmental amenities of their own area. Whenever there was an encroachment, they protested, often without success. They became increasingly aware of the real threat to Oxshott from increased traffic and building developers. James Shaw, Chairman of Bevendean Residents' Association, realising that a parochial approach could not protect the whole of the Oxshott area, set up meetings in 1987 with other residents' associations to see if they shared the same concerns. The general consensus was to have an overall organisation which could speak and act on behalf of all. A federal structure was preferred which, with grass root connections with residents through their individual associations, would be able to co-ordinate a unified plan of action and speak on behalf of all. Since some areas did not have an association, it was agreed that provision would be made for such residents to join the Federation individually and be represented on its Management Committee.

The first formal meeting of the Federation of Oxshott Residents Associations was on Tuesday, 29 March 1988 at Mr Shaw's home in Goldrings Road when the following provisional appointments were made: J. F. Shaw (Chairman), Dr B. S. Gidvani (Deputy Chairman), Edward Holding (Hon Treasurer) and Mrs Anne Holding (Hon Secretary). These appointments were confirmed with the addition of Wing Commander E. Kirby as Vice-Chairman at the first Annual General Meeting on 20 September 1989 at the Oxshott Village Centre.

Such was the interest of residents that the meeting hall was filled to capacity. Councillor John Trevena, Chairman of Elmbridge Borough Council's Planning Committee, addressed the meeting and fielded a battery of questions.

Right from the start, FEDORA set out to build important and useful contacts with local and national authorities, local and county councillors, Members of Parliament, residents' associations in neighbouring areas, other regulatory authorities and groups interested in the protection of the environment, such as Evergreen, the Elmbridge Green Belt and Urban Open Space Association. FEDORA is now a well-established organisation, supported and appreciated by residents of Oxshott for what it has done and is doing, to protect their village. It has developed into such an influential and powerful force that Elmbridge and Surrey County Councils take serious note of its views and often seeks its advice on matters affecting the village.

In 1994, FEDORA amended its name slightly to the Federation of Oxshott Residents *and* Associations to reflect more accurately membership of individuals and residents' associatons. Its current officers are Graham Clarke (Chairman), Ted Kirby (Deputy Chairman), David Cooke (Hon Secretary) and Councillor Norman Kaphan (Hon Treasurer). 165

ABOVE: Scouts' Memorial at Polyapes. BELOW: The
Oxshott Club.

ABOVE: Cricket Grounds with pavilions. BELOW:
Oxshott Football Team, 1928.

167

LEFT: Denise Wren. RIGHT: Rosemary Wren watched
by students of Royal Kent School, c1952. BELOW: Occa's
Corner today.

168

OCCA'S CORNER

Oxshott's original name was *Occa's Sceat*, meaning Occa's corner. Why he chose this particular location is unknown, but its beauty is. Occa would know that the hilly terrain amid miles of woods, with potential productive meadows, rich pasture and arable land, excellent springs, ponds and rivulets, could sustain a small colony and could be defended against enemy attack, but he could not have known that he was choosing one of the healthiest places in Surrey in which to live.

Louis Verrey, a resident of Leatherhead, came to live at the Warren on the recommendation of his doctor that his delicate daughter might benefit from the clean air of hilly Oxshott. Several residents of Oxshott have lived to a ripe age. Mrs Ada Sanders of Folgen, Sheath Lane, was still polishing the brass at St Andrew's at the age of 98 having started it soon after the end of the 1939-45 war. She passed away in 1969 aged 102. Her daughter, Joyce Sanders, lived to 94. Mrs Dival of Groom's Cottage, too, reached 102. Mrs Agnes Noon of Heathway was 101 when she died in 1966. Her daughter was 94 at her death. Kate Ayling was 96 and still writing poems. Eventually she went aged 97. Mrs Hackett of Crispin Cottage was 94½ years old at her death in 1995. Miss Hilda Crown of Steels Lane was 94 when she passed away.

In 1996 Dr J. R. A. (Hope) Madgwick of Gunters Mead, nearly 97, leads an active life and Mrs Eileen Parker at 96 is going strong. Mrs Pearl Smart of Broom Hall is 96½, playing bridge regularly and driving a car. Mrs Phyllis Harris and Commander Heathfield, both of Broom Hall, are 93 and 92 respectively. Oxshott has several other residents, including the writer, well past their mid-eighties.

Neither could Occa have known that so many well-known personalities from various walks of life would be attracted to make their home in his *Sceat*. Some have been mentioned and others include: authors John Montgomerey and Brigadier Lucas Phillips; Professor Gordon East and Dr D. M. A (Peter) Leggett, the first Vice Chancellor of Surrey University; British Railways' Chairman ('Butcher') Dr Beeching; champion golfer Colin Montgomerie; diplomats Sir John Moreton and Sir Duncan Watson; disk jockey David Hamilton, jazz musician Chris Barber; Olympic athlete and Granada Television Krypton Factor winner Ken Wilmshurst; Queen's Counsel Gerald Gardner; suffragette Mrs Despond.

It would also be strange if Oxshott did not have some eccentric, strong-willed persons. There was Bill Stacey. Nobody in Oxshott knew who he was or where he came from. He was an inoffensive person and kept aloof. He lived in a thick hedgerow near the top of the bridle path. He had made himself a shack out of railway sleepers and corrugated iron sheets with an open fire under a lean-to roof. He had a couple of dogs, one a greyhound. Bill had trained the dogs to catch rabbits which were in great abundance before myxomatosis wiped them out. He ate some and sold some which helped him to live a happy-go-lucky life. Occasionally he worked for the local Council, cutting back hedges and digging and filling ditches on the path from Wrens Hill to Blundel Lane.

Alan Simmons of Crown Cottages, Oxshott, when a young lad, had befriended Bill and remembers him with nostalgia. Alan once saw 'a city gent, complete with pinstripe suit and bowler hat' come trudging along the hedgerow to visit Bill. After inquiring about Bill's health, the gentleman put a wad of banknotes into his hand and was gone. Bill would not say who he was except that he met him while out walking and that the gentleman, always dressed like that, returned once a year to see that he was all right.

Bill had a good voice and his singing could be heard particularly on Sundays after lunch time lubrication. He had lived 50 years in Oxshott in that hut when he became ill. He was taken by an ambulance to Cobham Cottage Hospital where he died aged nearly 90.

Benny, as William Ben was usually called, was another loner, and did not talk about his background. It is believed he came from a decent well-to-do family and was jilted at the altar. He shunned company, but was friendly with children. He had a small grey beard and was well educated.

He had no money, but did not beg or complain. Yet he was always clean, decently dressed from cast-off clothes, and appeared well fed. He went to Reed's School for his breakfast and had whatever was left over. People liked him and gave him food and clothes, but he never showed any gratitude. He had emancipated himself forever from the need to care about such petty matters. He never worked nor felt any necessity for it. He lived simply in a hut at Scriven's Brick Works at the top of Donkey Lane (Knipp Hill), but sometimes slept under the trees in Oxshott Woods. He roamed the woods, often talking to himself loudly and felt he was master of the Heath. He always carried the few possessions he owned packed in a small suitcase. One day while walking in the woods, he was stopped by a plain clothes policeman and asked to open the suitcase. Ben was having none of it, struggled and was marched off to the police station. Poor Benny was convicted and sent to prison. People were upset and gave him a hero's welcome on his release.

When the Second World War came, food became scarce due to rationing and things were generally tight. Someone got him a ration card and collected a few shillings a week to keep him going. Then they got him an old age pension. Poor Ben, all of a sudden, felt rich and did not know what to do with all that money. He did not need any clothes as the prison authorities had given him a new outfit before release.

He went missing for a while. People were concerned and organised a search. He was found in his shack in the brickworks lying on a wooden plank covered with tattered blankets. Dr Lytle was called, diagnosed pneumonia and had him moved to a hospital in Guildford where after a few days he passed away peacefully.

For newcomers Oxshott's attraction is essentially due to its location — nearness to London, Heathrow and Gatwick — and its as yet unspoilt rural characteristics of a village amid hundreds of acres of beautiful and peaceful countryside.

Since most of the residential land was Crown property, development of the village has been at a controlled rate. Wisely, the Commissioners for Crown Lands at first opted for slow development and released land for building large mansions within extensive grounds. That prevented the clearance of vast areas of woodlands and preserved the rural aspect of the village.

With the arrival of the railway, getting to London became easier and quicker which attracted wealthy people to build houses for gracious living out of town. The mansions had lodges and cottages for their large retinue of twenty to thirty servants and provided recreational facilities. Most of the rich arrivals were public spirited and genuinely interested in the development of the village and the welfare of its residents. A great deal is due to the interest and activities of the first arrivals soon after the opening of Oxshott station. They donated land and money and their energy to build the essentials of any village — the school, the church, the village hall, men's and sports clubs. They were imbued with a strong sense of public duty and saw their civic duty as absolute, something owed to the community — to the village. It is hard to visualise what Oxshott would have been without the generosity and continuous efforts of the Ellises, the Eastwoods, the Lamberts, the Verreys, the Morrishes and others of that era.

Between the wars, more land was released for building individually designed smaller houses but still with large grounds to provide privacy and seclusion. They required fewer staff. By then a large number of the owners did not participate in community affairs. However, during and after the end of the 1939-45 war, there was a revival of community spirit. Records of that time show the great pride felt in the village and the amount of time, energy and money residents contributed to their community.

Oxshott in the 1950s remained largely the village it was before the Second World War; the building of post-war houses on leasehold plots with a minimum building cost of £1,300 had just started. Farming and brick-making disappeared and so did, for the most part, the large grounds attached to the tall Victorian houses. In general, gardens and orchards were converted into estates of another kind, housing estates. With the passage of time, the pace gathered, and by the eighties, most of the new houses have small manageable gardens.

Oxshott at one time was self-contained. The High Street had shops to provide all the essential requirements; not so now, but that is the way of modern life. Residents have to go outside the village to supermarkets in Esher, Cobham or Leatherhead for daily needs and variety.

Many people would query that Oxshott is any longer a village — more of a dormitory for commuters and part of the outer London sprawl. It is a sad fact that a majority of residents have to go out of the village for work, play and recreation, but a village atmosphere still prevails. Oxshott, though developed during the past 30-odd years, has still resisted that urbanisation and industrialisation which has destroyed most of the old rural charm of neighbouring Esher.

The village continues to grow — from a population of less than 500 in 1890 to just over 4,000 now. Developers have managed to get a foothold and are putting up more and more labour-saving compact luxury houses with small gardens. There are no 'start-up' houses for the young and social housing for the elderly. Where it will end is anybody's guess.

Oxshott is proud of its timeless history. Its charm and attractiveness lies in its environs and amenities. Their preservation is the sacred duty of its residents; the new residents to remember that these were the very reasons that brought them to the village and the older residents not to take the village for granted and to respond to the needs and problems that arise. According to the Duke of Edinburgh 'the difficulty is that the average commuter does not notice because it is only the older people who remember what it used to be. If people in this generation have any feelings whatever for their descendants, they ought to be a lot more active in the conservation of nature and in the conservation of its resources'.

Above all, there is still a friendliness and warmth in the majority of Oxshott residents and that sense of belonging and personal identity, which marks out the true English village.